Cambridge Elements ≡

Elements in the History of Constantinople
edited by
Peter Frankopan
University of Oxford

THE CHURCH OF ST. POLYEUKTOS AT CONSTANTINOPLE

Fabian Stroth
University of Freiburg

CAMBRIDGE
UNIVERSITY PRESS

CAMBRIDGE
UNIVERSITY PRESS

Shaftesbury Road, Cambridge CB2 8EA, United Kingdom

One Liberty Plaza, 20th Floor, New York, NY 10006, USA

477 Williamstown Road, Port Melbourne, VIC 3207, Australia

314–321, 3rd Floor, Plot 3, Splendor Forum, Jasola District Centre, New Delhi – 110025, India

103 Penang Road, #05–06/07, Visioncrest Commercial, Singapore 238467

Cambridge University Press is part of Cambridge University Press & Assessment, a department of the University of Cambridge.

We share the University's mission to contribute to society through the pursuit of education, learning and research at the highest international levels of excellence.

www.cambridge.org
Information on this title: www.cambridge.org/9781009517065

DOI: 10.1017/9781009105729

First published 2024

A catalogue record for this publication is available from the British Library.

ISBN 978-1-009-51706-5 Hardback
ISBN 978-1-009-10132-5 Paperback
ISSN 2514-3891 (online)
ISSN 2514-3883 (print)

The Church of St. Polyeuktos at Constantinople

Elements in the History of Constantinople

DOI: 10.1017/9781009105729
First published online: February 2024

Fabian Stroth
University of Freiburg

Author for correspondence: Fabian Stroth, fabian.stroth@iaw.uni-freiburg.de

Abstract: The Church of St. Polyeuktos is one of the most magnificent, but also most peculiar, architectural achievements in Byzantine Constantinople. The accidental rediscovery of the building during construction work in Istanbul in the 1960s is legendary and considered one of the most sensational finds in Byzantine archaeology. Built by the aristocrat Lady Anicia Juliana, the reconstruction of the structure and the interpretation of its strange forms continue to challenge scholars today.

The building gave rise to a whole series of archaeo-historical narratives, in which the City's Byzantine protagonists and major monuments were woven into a coherent plot.

This Element on the archaeology of St. Polyeuktos takes a closer look at these narratives and subjects them to critical examination. In the end, the study of St. Polyeuktos will tell us as much about Byzantine architectural history in the second half of the twentieth century as about early Byzantine architecture itself.

Keywords: Constantinople, Byzantium, architecture, archaeology, Justinian

ISBNs: 9781009517065 (HB), 9781009101325 (PB), 9781009105729 (OC)
ISSNs: 2514-3891 (online), 2514-3883 (print)

Contents

1 The Rediscovery   1

2 The Foundress Anicia Juliana   6

3 The Early Churches of Constantinople   11

4 The Dating   20

5 The Site   21

6 The Epigrams   29

7 The Architectural Sculpture   39

8 The Reconstructions   44

9 No Temple for Byzantium   55

10 The Site in the Middle Ages   60

   Bibliography   66

1 The Rediscovery

During road construction work in the Saraçhane quarter of Istanbul in the spring of 1960, builders accidentally unearthed elaborately and inscribed marble blocks. These blocks, it turned out, were parts of St. Polyeuktos Church.

However, this often-told story of the serendipitous find is not as neat as the anecdote suggests. In fact, the discovery had its starting points some 350 years earlier, far away from the Bosporus in the small university town of Heidelberg, Germany. As early as 1606, the French scholar Claude Saumaise came across an unknown Byzantine codex in the Palatine Library in Heidelberg, a codex which is now known around the globe as the *Anthologia Palatina*.[1] This collection of more than 3500 Greek epigrams was compiled in Constantinople in the tenth century. The manuscript is of particular importance for Byzantine archaeology as it preserves the epigrams of 123 buildings and artifacts of Constantinople, most of which are lost today.[2] Among them are complete copies of the two dedicatory epigrams of the church of St. Polyeuktos (Figure 1). Only because of the medieval record, handwritten on two sheets of parchment, was it possible to identify and to reconstruct the material remains of one of the largest and most extravagant Byzantine churches in the City. In archaeology, small clues often turn out to be keys to the bigger picture. This is especially true for the archaeology of St. Polyeuktos Church.

When the marble blocks of the church were discovered in 1960, the find spread like wildfire in academic circles (Figure 2). Scholars quickly understood their significance. Ihor Ševčenko and Cyril Mango immediately associated the relief letters carved in marble with the ink writing in the Heidelberg manuscript:[3] the famous Church of St. Polyeuktos, set up by Theodosian princess Anicia Juliana in the capital of the Roman world, Constantinople, had been rediscovered.[4] Its chance finding is considered one of the most important discoveries in Byzantine archaeology to date.

An excavation of the site was clearly warranted. The Image Collection and Fieldwork Archives at Dumbarton Oaks and the Saraçhane Excavation Archive at the University of Oxford hold correspondence that vividly documents the start of this important project. Shortly after the discovery of the inscribed marble blocks, on November 1, 1960, the director of Dumbarton Oaks, Paul

---

[1] Heidelberg, University Library, Cod. Pal. Graec. 23. See Bauer, "christlichen Gedichten"; Cameron, *Greek Anthology*; van Dienten, "Herstellung des Codex Palat."; Agosti and Gonnelli, "Materiali per la storia dell'esametro."

[2] Connor, "Epigram in the Church"; Pizzone, "Da Melitene a Costantinopoli"; Whitby, "Vocabulary of Praise"; Whitby, "The St. Polyeuktos Epigram."

[3] Ševčenko, "Note additionnelle"; Dirimtekin, "Finds from the Site"; Mango and Ševčenko, "Remains of the Church," 243–248.

[4] Peschlow, "Review of Harrison 1989," 628.

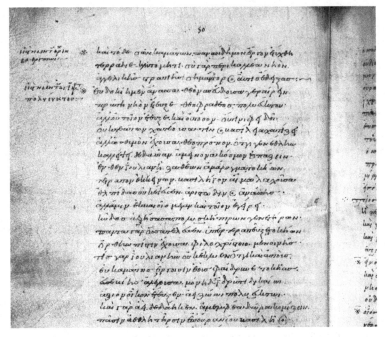

Figure 1 The *Anthologia Palatina* (tenth century) contains full copies of the two epigrams of St. Polyeuktos (Credit: Heidelberg, University library, Codex Palatinus Graecus 23, 1.10)

Figure 2 Great entablature with remains of the dedicatory epigram, accidentally brought to light by a bulldozer in 1960 (Credit: Saraçhane Excavation Archive, University of Oxford)

Underwood, wrote to his colleagues Ernest Hawkins and Ercüment Atabay, who were residing in Istanbul at the time:

> I am writing to you jointly asking that you seek information and advice from various people with regard to the possibility of obtaining permission for the Byzantine Institute to excavate the site where the architectural fragments were discovered at Saraçhane. We would like very much to do this [. . .]. First let me state some of the reasons why we want to do this job and do it now. We know now the identification of the church from which the fragments come, thanks to Sevcenko and Mango. (Incidentally, I think it would be unwise at present to let it be known that the identification, and date, which are absolutely certain, have been established. If, however it becomes necessary, as a means of impressing on the authorities the importance of the building from the archaeological point of view, it might be wise simply to state that these things are known). In any case, and to partially satisfy your curiosity, the monument was a very important one from various reasons. First, it represents a building of a period in the development of Byzantine architecture that is very little known and which was surely a turning point in that development since it was a transitional phase. It forms in plan, superstructure, and interior decoration may well turn out to be unique among known churches.[5]

History would prove him right. However, the first project proposals were rejected several times by the Turkish authorities, and it took almost four years until they finally succeeded in obtaining permission for the work. Even before the permit was granted, Dumbarton Oaks started looking for people to take charge of the project; an early enquiry went to David Oates (Cambridge)[6] and later to Peter Megaw (Athens),[7] John B. Ward Perkins (Rome),[8] and Martin Harrison, then lecturer at the University of Newcastle upon Tyne.[9] On June 1, 1964, the long-awaited letter of confirmation by Necati Dolunay, then director of the Archaeological Museum in Istanbul, arrived:

> This excavation will be as important to the topography of Istanbul as it is to the early Byzantine art and archaeology. [. . .] I have received the oral agreement of our Department of Archaeology for this joint excavation. [. . .] The Archaeological Museum will obtain the necessary permission from all authorities concerned, and that it would represent both parties in

---

[5] Letter by P. Underwood to Ernest Hawkins and Ercüment Atabay, November 1, 1960, ICFA Dumbarton Oaks (MS.BZ.004.01.01, Box 13, Folder 182).

[6] Letter by E. Kitzinger to David Oates, January, 4 1962 and the kind refusal by Oates to Kitzinger, December, 15, 1962, ICFA Dumbarton Oaks (MS.BZ.004.01.01, Box 15, Folder 219).

[7] Letter by P. Underwood to A. H. W. Megaw, January 13, 1964, ICFA Dumbarton Oaks (MS. BZ.004.01.01, Box 15, Folder 219).

[8] Letter by P. Underwood to J. B. Ward Perkins, January 13, 1964, ICFA Dumbarton Oaks (MS. BZ.004.01.01, Box 15, Folder 219).

[9] Letter by P. Underwood to M. Harrison, February 4, 1964, ICFA Dumbarton Oaks (MS. BZ.004.01.01, Box 15, Folder 219)

dealing with all municipal and state laws and regulations. [...] The excavation must be directed both by Mr. R. M. Harrison and by the director of the Archaeological Museums of Istanbul or his representative with the same and mutual rights.[10]

Finally Dumbarton Oaks was able to get the permission and to establish a joint leadership with Martin Harrison as excavation director and Nezih Fıratlı as representative of the Museum in Istanbul. Ernst Kitzinger was soon taken with the way Harrison managed the project and sought to hire him permanently as a lecturer in Byzantine archaeology and director of fieldwork at Dumbarton Oaks. A tempting offer, which Harrison gratefully declined for family reasons.[11]

In 1964 the project could finally start.[12] The excavation was carried out in six campaigns, dating from 1964 to 1969, with excavators publishing preliminary results in annual reports and numerous articles.[13] When the two final monographs were published twenty years after the excavations began, the interest of the academic community remained undiminished. Harrison's work was considered exemplary, and the book received an exceptionally high number of reviews.[14]

The excavation set new standards for the archaeology of Istanbul in many respects. The stratigraphic method used was innovative for the time and applied strictly. Equally careful attention was paid to the recording and evaluation of small finds, like pottery, coins, and bones. Unfortunately, the same cannot be said for the documentation and interpretation of the architecture itself.

When the first marble blocks in the Saraçhane quarter came to light, it was suddenly possible to recognize architectural sculptures which had been used in very different places as original components of St. Polyeuktos. Scholars were not surprised to find decorated fragments of the church reused as *spolia* in several of Istanbul's mosques, such as the Mola Zeyrek Camii (former Monastery of the Pantokrator),[15] the Fenari Isa Camii (former Monastery of

---

[10] Letter by N. Dolunay to P. Underwood, June 1, 1964, ICFA Dumbarton Oaks (MS.BZ.004.01.01, Box 15, Folder 219).

[11] Letter by E. Kitzinger to M. Harrison, October 28, 1965; Harrisons kind refusal, November 8, 1965 and the reply by Kitzinger, November 15, 1965. Saraçhane Excavation Archive, University of Oxford.

[12] Parpulov and Schachner, *From the Bosporus to Oxford*, p. 1.

[13] Harrison and Fıratlı, "First Preliminary Report", "Second and Third Preliminary Reports," "Fourth Preliminary Reports," "Fifth Preliminary Report"; Harrison, "Excavations 1964," "Excavations 1965," "Excavations 1966," "Discoveries 1964–1965," "Excavation Report," "Discoveries," "Excavations 1968," "Sculptural Decoration," "Constantinopolitan Capital," "Scavi della chiesa," "Anicia Juliana's Church," "Church of St. Polyeuktos."

[14] Harrison, *Excavations, vol. 1*, and *Temple for Byzantium*; Hayes, *Excavations, vol. II*; Reviews by Hodges, Lafontaine, Vickers, Spieser, Gregory, Hill, Koder, Mango, Smith, Peschlow, Arthur, François, Kaegi, Terry, Warmebol.

[15] Van Millingen, *Byzantine Churches*, p. 238, pl. 67; Megaw, "Notes on Recent Work," 346, fig. 8; Harrison and Fıratlı, "Fourth Preliminary Report," 276, fig. 12; Harrison, *Temple for Byzantium*,

Lips),[16] the Davut Pasha Camii,[17] and the Koça Mustafa Pasha Camii (former Monastery of St. Andrew in Krisei).[18] Similarly unsurprising was the recognition of corresponding pieces from St. Polyeuktos in the collection of the Istanbul Archaeological Museum, which had already been found in the early twentieth century at Topkapı Sarayı,[19] the Edirnekapı,[20] in the Saraçhane quarter,[21] and three fragments more recently refound in the Mangana region.[22]

More astounding was the identification of corresponding architectural components in more distant places such as Venice,[23] Milan,[24] Vienna,[25] and even Barcelona.[26] After the sack of Constantinople by the Crusaders in 1204, the marbles were shipped to the Western Mediterranean and incorporated into illustrious local narratives of cultural appropriation.[27] The most famous of these wandering stones are undoubtedly the so-called *pilastri acritani* in front of the southern façade of San Marco in Venice (Figure 3). In the City's communal memory, the pillars were actively reinterpreted as trophies of a victory in Acre – an important city for the Crusaders in the Holy Land – over the rival city-state of Genoa.[28] It was not until the twentieth century that the excavations in Istanbul disproved this medieval propaganda.

This "archaeological detective story"[29] of the rediscovery of St. Polyeuktos along with its objects' itineraries, now found in several cities of Mediterranean Europe, certainly provides one of the most spectacular backdrops of Byzantine architectural heritage.

While the rediscovery and excavation of St. Polyeuktos in Istanbul was without doubt one of the greatest sensations of Byzantine archaeology in the

---

p. 106, fig. 126; Barsanti and Pilutti Namer, "Da Costantinopoli a Venezia," 143n34; Flamine, *Opere d'arte bizantina*, p. 78.

[16] Megaw, "Notes on Recent Work"; Harrison and Fıratlı, "Fourth Preliminary Report"; Ousterhout, "Study and Restoration."

[17] Guidobaldi, "Scultura costantinopolitana," 231–244.

[18] Harrison and Fıratlı, "Second and Third Preliminary Reports"; Harrison, *Temple for Byzantium*, p. 101, fig. 119.

[19] Ebersolt, *Mission archéologique*, p. 4, pl. 24, 3.

[20] Aşgari, "Edirnekapı Başlığı," 14–17; Harrison, *Temple for Byzantium*, p. 116, fig. 117.

[21] Mendel, *Catalogue des sculptures*, pp. 466–467, no. 1242; Fıratlı, *Sculpture byzantine figurée*, pp. 115–116, no. 215.

[22] Tunay, "Byzantine Archaeological Findings," 223–224, fig. 10.

[23] Deichmann, "Pilastri acritani," 75–89; Deichmann, *Corpus der Kapitelle*, pp, 138–141; Peschlow, "Dekorative Plastik," 406–417; Vickers, "A 'New' Capital"; Barsanti, "Venezia e Costantinopoli"; Barsanti and Pilutti Namer, 'Da Costantinopoli a Venezia'; Meier, *Spolien*, pp. 43–44.

[24] Bertelli, "Spigolature bizantine," "Transenna frammentaria"; Bertelli, "Lastra scolpita," 42–43.

[25] Vickers, "Sixth-Century Byzantine Source"; Harrison, "Anicia Juliana's Church," 435–439.

[26] Schlunk, "Byzantinische Bauplastik," 235–236; Harrison, "Excavation Report," 543–549; Harrison, "Constantinopolitan Capital"; Singes, "Archivo gráfico," 3–10.

[27] Perry, "Saint Mark's Trophies"; Vickers, "Wandering Stones"; Tigler, "Pilastri 'acritani'"; Tronzo, "Reading the Display."

[28] Nelson, "High Justice"; Nelson, "History of Legends."   [29] Runciman, "Preface," 8.

Figure 3 The so-called *pilastri acritani* next to San Marco in Venice. These
pillars originate from St. Polyeuktos, brought to the West after 1204
(Credit: M. Pellegrin 2019)

twentieth century, the scholarly expectations for this find were completely
exaggerated. Many thought that this building would act as a missing link and
would be able to explain the many open questions about the innovations in
early-sixth-century Constantinopolitan architecture. However, St. Polyeuktos
hardly provided any answers, but raised more questions than it answered.

The building gradually gave rise to a whole series of archaeo-historical
narratives that became more and more established over the decades, in which
the City's important Byzantine protagonists and the surviving major monuments were woven into a coherent plot. This Element on the archaeology of
St. Polyeuktos must necessarily take a closer look at these narratives and subject
them to critical examination. In the end, the study of St. Polyeuktos will tell us
as much about Byzantine architectural history in the second half of the twentieth
century as about early Byzantine architecture itself.

2 The Foundress Anicia Juliana

Born around the year 463, the foundress of St. Polyeuktos, Anicia Juliana, was an
aristocrat with a formidable genealogy. Her father, Flavius Anicius Olybrius, was
one of the last legitimate emperors of the West whose family was from that

ancient and most noble Roman *gens*, the Anicii.[30] Her mother's line was no less impressive; both grandparents were directly descended from Emperor Theodosius I, and her mother herself was the daughter of Emperor Valentinian III.

In 479, at about sixteen years of age, Juliana was offered in marriage to Theodoric the Great by Emperor Zeno. Though this marriage did not take place, she was married to Flavius Areobindus Dagalaifus soon thereafter. With him she had only one son, Flavius Anicius Olybrios Junior, who was consul in the East as a very young boy in 491. In November 512 – the year of the presumed start of construction of the Church of St. Polyeuktos – a rebelling Chalcedonian crowd proclaimed Juliana's husband Areobindus as counter-emperor in front of her palace. Areobindus, however, evaded the emperorship by fleeing, thereby proving his loyalty to the emperor Anastasius.[31]

As the last living female member of the Theodosian dynasty and the daughter of a former emperor, she was the only one in Constantinople at the time to hold the title of *Nobilissima Patrikia* (ἐπιφανεστάτη πατρικία), which denotes the highest rank for a woman belonging to the imperial family. Juliana is generally assumed to have died in the year 528 and therefore only lived to witness the first year of Justinian's sole reign.

The only portrait of Anicia Juliana that we know of is the famous dedicatory miniature of the Vienna *Dioscurides*, a sixth-century scientific manuscript.[32] This book is related to Julianas' role as a *building tycoon* of the City and was presented to her out of gratitude for her foundation of another church in the suburbs of Constantinople already in 515 CE.[33] The miniature shows Juliana in an imperial pose distributing donations.[34] She is flanked by personifications of Magnanimity, Prudence, and Gratitude of the Arts. Of particular interest for architectural history are the small grisailles in the outer spandrels of the frame, which show typical activities on a Late Antique construction site.[35]

Was There a Personal Rivalry between Juliana and Justinian?

Many scholars believe that a great rivalry existed between the foundress of St. Polyeuktos, Anicia Juliana, and the founder of Hagia Sophia, Emperor Justinian, and that this rivalry was one of the driving forces for both of these spectacular architectural achievements.[36] Indeed, these two characters appear to

---

[30] Viermann, "Surpassing Solomon," 216–218.   [31] Meier, "Der Aufstand."

[32] Cod. Vind. med. gr. 1, fol. 6v. A bust often associated with Anicia Juliana in MET Cloisters Collection, Inv. 66.25, does not depict the princess. Harrison, *Temple for Byzantium*, p. 39.

[33] Gamillscheg, "Geschenk für Juliana Anicia."

[34] Diez, "Miniaturen des Wiener Dioskurides"; Kiilerich, "Reconsidering Figural Marble Panels."

[35] Diez, "Miniaturen des Wiener Dioskurides," 27.

[36] Harrison, *Temple for Byzantium*, p. 40; Koder, "Justinians Sieg," 135–142; Ousterhout, "New Temples and New Solomons," 243; Meier, *Justinian*, 256–257; Talbot, "Patronage," 169.

be the perfect antagonists in this historical screenplay. On the one side we find the high-born aristocrat Anicia Juliana, whose family was one of the most illustrious in the Roman Empire and whose epigrams in St. Polyeuktos testify to the highest level of classical education. On the other side stands Emperor Justinian, who was often portrayed as a lowborn social climber from the provinces and whose proficiency in the Greek language was weak, if we believe Procopius' accusations.

Scholars believe that Anicia Juliana built the church of St. Polyeuktos as a visual reminder in the cityscape of Constantinople that the Theodosian house was a serious rival to the ruling authority in both the political and religious spheres.[37] The two dedicatory poems of St. Polyeuktos insistently refer to the imperial lineage of Anicia Juliana and are commonly understood to question the authority of the emperor (see Section 6). Indeed, the Anicii were part of the highest society and were a family of such prestige that they could well have provided an emperor. However, this storyline presents some chronological issues. If one accepts the early dating for the beginning of the construction of St. Polyeuktos in the years 512/13, as Jonathan Bardill has convincingly shown on the basis of the evidence drawn from brick stamps, Justinian cannot have been the initial target of such a political project. At that time, after all, Emperor Anastasius I still resided in the imperial palace, to whom Juliana and her husband Areobindus were loyal. There is no historical evidence for the common scholarly conviction that Juliana hoped to elevate her son to the throne as emperor after the death of Anastasios.[38] Moreover, the election of Justin I and the elevation of Justinian to co-Augustus in 527 would have put an abrupt end to such hopes if they had indeed existed. Finally, there would have been very little time for a rivalry to unfold between Juliana and Emperor Justinian, as she died only a year after his coronation in 528.

A small group of textual sources is generally cited as evidence of an alleged rivalry between Juliana and Justinian. The first consists of the enkomion in Juliana's church and the epigram in the church of Sts. Sergius and Bacchus, Justinian and Theodora's first foundation as the reigning imperial couple. The latter is often interpreted as the court's response to the provoking poems in St. Polyeuktos.[39] If this was true, though, this much shorter epigram in this much smaller church would have been a very restrained imperial reply; for this

---

[37] Bardill, "A New Temple," 340.

[38] Effenberger, "'Sasanidischer' Baudekor in Byzanz," 161 n69.

[39] Connor, "Epigram in the Church," 511; Bardill, "Church of Sts. Sergius and Bacchus," 4; Shahîd, "The Church of Sts. Sergios and Bakchos," 476–480; Croke, "Justinian, Theodora, and the Church," 50; Whitby, "The St. Polyeuktos Epigram"; Ousterhout, "New Temples and New Solomons," 247; Agosti 2018, 685; Leatherbury, *Inscribing Faith*, p. 150.

reason alone, this evidence is unconvincing. The compared epigrams work very differently in the architectural space and the references made are of a very general nature.[40] Both poems address similar themes like piety, toil, and labor, which is not surprising in dedicatory epigrams from this time and location.[41] If we look at the epigrams from an archaeological perspective and understand them as stone masonry, the idea of one responding to the other becomes far-fetched (see Section 6).

In Gregory of Tours' *De Gloria Martyrum*, the sixth-century Frankish chronicler tells an oft-cited story of how Juliana tricked Justinian, who sought to deprive her of her riches, by casting all of her gold into plaques that were affixed to the ceiling of her new basilica.[42] This anecdote is not only of archaeological interest for the reconstruction of the roof of the church of St. Polyeuktos (see Section 8) but is also seen as evidence of the rivalry between the two. As the story goes, Justinian learned of Juliana's wealth and decided to approach her for a donation to the imperial treasury. Juliana managed to stall the emperor in order to "conceal what she had consecrated to God."[43] She summoned craftsmen and asked them to cover the church's ceiling with the rest of her gold "so that the hand of this greedy emperor w[ould] not touch [the gold]."[44] Arriving at Juliana's church with the expect-ation that he would receive a great fortune, Justinian understood that he had been tricked by her. Hiding his embarrassment, the emperor gave thanks and let Juliana placate him with a small gold ring.

It is not easy to determine the credibility of this text, written in distant France, half a century after the encounter, and by an author who had never visited Constantinople himself.[45] Though it contains some information that is generally considered correct about the shape and location of the famous church, the passage of Anicia Juliana's encounter with the emperor makes use of a very popular topos, namely, the greedy tax collector Justinian.[46]

That this topos of "Kaiserkritik" against Justinian as a greedy yet easily fooled emperor enjoyed long-lasting popularity, at least in the West, can be seen in an episode in Agnellus' *Liber Pontificalis Ecclesiae Ravennatis*.[47] The ninth-century chronicler begins his chapter on Bishop Maximian with an

---

[40] Stroth, *Monogrammkapitelle*, pp. 86–91, pp. 102–110.

[41] Connor, "Epigram in the Church," 511–512.

[42] GM 102, pp. 105–107; see Cutler, "Perils of Polyeuktos," 92; Rotman, "Hagiography, Historiography, and Identity," 82–86.

[43] GM 102, p. 106.   [44] Ibid.

[45] Cameron, "Byzantine Sources of Gregory"; Rotman, "Hagiography, Historiography, and Identity."

[46] Procopius, *Anekdota*, 8.   [47] Deliyannis, *Agnelli Ravennatis*.

interesting, but lesser-known, anecdote on how the latter obtained the emperor's support for his election to become bishop of Ravenna.[48]

> One day when Maximian was digging in the earth, [...] he suddenly found a large vase filled with gold and many other kinds of riches. He, thinking to himself that it could not remain hidden, ordered a great cow to be brought and killed, and he commanded that its stomach, emptied of muck, be filled with gold coins. Likewise he summoned the cobblers, who made foot coverings, and commanded them to produce great boots from the skins of goats, and he filled these with gold solidi. He brought the remainder with him when he went to the city of Constantinople, and gave it to the Emperor Justinian. When the emperor saw it, after thanking him he inquired searchingly if there was more. But Maximian, under oath, answered the emperor: "By your health, lord, and by the salvation of your soul, I do not have more of it than what I lavished on stomach and boots." The emperor thought that he spoke of food for the body and coverings for the feet; Maximian of course was referring to that which he had hidden. Justinian considered what sort of reward he should give for such faith as Maximian had shown him.[49]

In Agnellus' story again, the image of the money-grubbing Justinian is used, who allows himself to be cheated by a tricky protagonist. We can conclude for the earlier work of Gregory of Tour, that the anecdote of Juliana and Justinian does not aim to inform us about the relationship or rivalry between the two protagonists nor to give any art-historical information about the roof of St. Polyeuktos. Gregory's book is first of all a hagiographical work that makes use of this captivating narrative to tell a miracle story about his main figure, the holy martyr Polyeuktos. The Frankish author concludes his account as follows:

> Whence there is no doubt, that the virtue of the martyr interceded even in this matter, to prevent the transference of wealth which had been earmarked for holy places and for poor, into the control of a man, by whose efforts it had not been acquired.[50]

Even if we consider that Gregory probably had access to Byzantine sources, we should be cautious about reading the text as an account reflective of the genuine reality of sixth-century Constantinople.[51] Much as we would like to, we certainly cannot accept it as a record of an instance of personal bickering between Juliana and Justinian.[52]

Justinian's famous line when he first entered the rebuilt Hagia Sophia is also often quoted to link the alleged rivalry between the two to their church foundations.

---

[48] Nauerth, *Liber Pontificalis*, vol. I, p. 26, p. 70, pp. 300–301.
[49] Deliyannis, *The book of Pontiffs*, 184–185.   [50] GM 102, p. 107.
[51] Cameron, "Byzantine Sources of Gregory."
[52] Critical comments on the credibility of this passage: Bardill *Brickstamps, vol I*, 112.

His phrase "Solomon, I have defeated you!" (ἐνίκησά σε Σολομῶν)[53] is transmitted through the *Diegesis*, a notoriously inaccurate ninth-century source referenced frequently, but with too little skepticism.[54] This medieval anecdote is understood by scholars not only as an allusion to the biblical First Temple, but also as the emperor's rival response to Anicia Juliana and her Church of St. Polyeuktos, which is thought to be a copy of the Temple (see Section 9). Robert Ousterhout would even like to detect a pun here: Ἐνίκησά / Ἀνικία.[55] However, if references to Solomon can be traced to two churches built in Constantinople at about the same time, this is, first of all, not an expression of rivalry but an indication of similarity.[56] During those days, references to Solomon and his Temple were a topos of Christian rhetoric and occur quite frequently in early Byzantine building epigrams and ekphrases.[57] There is no good reason for historians to construct a double entendre here. If Justinian really uttered this sentence – which is more than doubtful – it was hardly in reply to St. Polyeuktos.

It is beyond question that, by founding prestigious and monumental churches, Anicia Juliana and Emperor Justinian both intended to make striking statements of power and authority. However, it is far less certain that the driving force for these large-scale projects was a personal rivalry between these two protagonists.[58] To reduce architectural achievements like the churches of St. Polyeuktos, Sts. Sergius and Bacchus, and Hagia Sophia to an imperial squabble is a double misunderstanding; it not only underestimates the complexity of early Byzantine architectural history but also trivializes the dynamic social relations of Late Antique Constantinople.

3 The Early Churches of Constantinople

It is not easy to make sense of the Church of St. Polyeuktos in relation to early Byzantine architectural history. On the one hand, the building is considered to be a key monument to one of the most experimental periods of Eastern Medieval building. On the other, though ostentatious in its decoration, it was in many ways a conservative building that looked backward rather than forward.

The Church of St. Polyeuktos has often been discussed in relation to the slightly later erected Justinianic churches in Constantinople and has often been referred to as the predecessor or even prototype of Hagia Sophia.[59]

---

[53] *Narratio de S. Sophia* 27, ed. Berger, *Patria*, 266–267.   [54] Berger, *Patria*, xvii–xviii.

[55] Ousterhout, "Aesthetics and Politics," 110; Ousterhout, "New Temples and New Solomons," 245.

[56] Hill, "Review of Harrison 1989," 253; Connor, "Epigram in the Church," 480.

[57] Koder, "Justinians Sieg," 135–138; Ousterhout, "New Temples and New Solomons."

[58] Harrison, *Excavations, vol. I*, 408–409.

[59] Ousterhout, *Eastern Medieval Architecture*, p. 182; Stroth, *Monogrammkapitelle*, p. 100.

This evolutionary perspective has also caused scholars to reconstruct the building with a central dome, despite excavations indicating a ground plan with a clear basilical shape and showing no evidence of a dome (see also Section 8).[60] In fact, it would not be appropriate to consider the building a precursor of the innovations of Justinianic architecture; neither the interior arrangement nor the outlandish sculpture of the church seems to have served as a model for Byzantine architecture of the following years and decades. Indeed, the architectural experiment of St. Polyeuktos remained a dead end for Byzantine building in many respects.

It is therefore worthwhile to leave Justinian's Hagia Sophia aside for a moment and to consider the great basilicas of the City that already existed at the time when St. Polyeuktos was designed. This is easier said than done, since the archaeological evidence for most of these early basilicas is very limited.[61] Nevertheless, the archaeological finds, together with the written sources, provide at least a limited picture of fifth-century church-building in Constantinople.

The Great Basilicas of the City in the Fifth Century

The Old Hagia Sophia, the predecessor of Justinian's Great Church, was inaugurated in the year 415 CE as a replacement for an even older church building that stood on the same site.[62] When the church of St. Polyeuktos was built, the cathedral of Constantinople was already 100 years old but remained the largest ecclesiastical building in the capital. Its founder was Anicia Juliana's great-grandfather, Emperor Theodosius II, whose name also appears prominently in the epigram on the western façade of St. Polyeuktos and whose wife Eudocia is praised in the *naos* epigram as the foundress of the latter's predecessor.

We have only limited information about the actual design of Old Hagia Sophia, but we can reconstruct its essential features thanks to textual sources and excavations by Alfons Maria Schneider that brought to light parts of its western entrance.[63] The main portal of the church was integrated into the portico of a colonnaded street that ran west of the church (Figure 4). A richly decorated propylon within the portico drew attention to the entrance of the church's atrium.[64] A colossal portal, more than four meters wide and equipped with door frames made of striking red stone, was set into the wall behind this

---

[60] Harrison, *Excavations, vol. I*, p. 408.   [61] Still groundbreaking Mathews, *Early Churches*.

[62] Comprehensive Taddei *Hagia Sophia*; For the dating see Bardill, *Brickstamps*, p. 107.

[63] Schneider 1941, 3–22; Mathews, *Early Churches*, pp. 11–19; Russo, "Sculptural Decoration," 19–34; Taddei, *Hagia Sophia*, 135–228.

[64] For the sculpture, see Deichmann, *Studien*, 63–69 and Russo, "Sculptural Decoration."

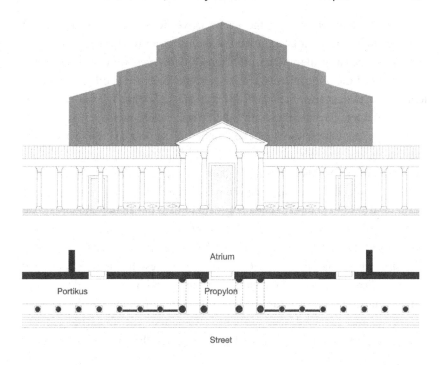

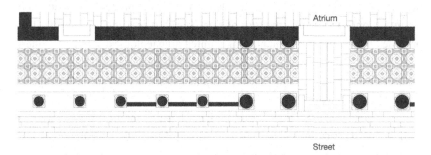

Figure 4 The west façade and the entrance area of the Old Hagia Sophia (Credit: Drawing by D. Miznazi 2022 after Schneider 1941)

propylon.[65] Two relief friezes, each showing a row of six lambs, were part of the inner architrave of the propylon and ran toward the tympanum above the main portal. These reliefs are of importance for us, since they imply the existence of

---

[65] Schneider, *Grabung*, 5. 16, fig. 6–7; Taddei, *Hagia Sophia*, 191.

an original figural decoration in the lunette above the entrance.[66] As for the size of the entire complex, a lateral portal in the rear wall of the portico gives an approximate idea of the width of the church. However, we only have vague indications of the original length. A proportional reconstruction can nevertheless be assumed, at least hypothetically. Old Hagia Sophia is generally reconstructed as a five-nave basilica with galleries and an atrium in the west. In both complexes, the dimensions would be roughly the same, about 50 meters wide and 100 meters long (Figure 5).[67]

The Church of the Theotokos in Chalkoprateia (Figure 5) was situated within 150 meters of Old Hagia Sophia and contained the most important shrine of the Virgin in Constantinople.[68] Scholars generally date the church roughly to the mid-fifth century, but poor preservation prevents a reliable dating or reconstruction of the building. We know it was a three-aisled basilica with a polygonal apse, a narthex, and an atrium. Of particular interest for us is a connected structure located north of the church's atrium. As with St. Polyeuktos, since only the substructures have survived, the superstructure of this smaller building cannot be reconstructed with certainty. Here, too, the foundation shows a conspicuous footing in the center. This is generally understood to act as a support for the piscina of a baptistery above, since a monolithic piscina was found on the site.[69]

Founded in the mid-fifth century, the Church of St. John Stoudios is the oldest surviving church in Constantinople (Figure 5). The building is often considered the archetype of the City's classical basilicas, which is probably also due to it being the only surviving structure of this type.[70] It is a three-naved basilica preceded by a narthex and an atrium. Limited archaeological sondages undertaken by Urs Peschlow in the 1970s suggest that this courtyard had a sloping western course to account for a street lying in front of it, similar to the situation west of St. Polyeuktos.[71]

When compared to St. Polyeuktos, the early basilicas of the City offer a set of comparable characteristics, but also significant differences. All churches had western courtyards and almost square floor plans for naos and aisles together; all had galleries and wooden roofing which was the standard solution for these buildings. The dimensions of St. Polyeuktos are also quite comparable to those of Old Hagia Sophia, making the building one of the largest churches in the City

---

[66] Schneider, *Grabung*, 12; Taddei, *Hagia Sophia*.

[67] Nathan, "Architectural Narratology," 443.

[68] Kleiss, "Neue Befunde"; Kleiss, "Grabungen"; Mathews, *Early Churches*, 28–33.

[69] Schneider, "vorjustinianische Sophienkirche," 56; Kleiss, "Neue Befunde," 164

[70] Ousterhout, *Eastern Medieval Architecture*, 39–41; Kudde, "Construction and Architectural Characteristics," 22–34; Marinis, "Church Building," 182.

[71] Peschlow, "Johanneskirche," 432; Bardill, *Brickstamps*, p. 61.

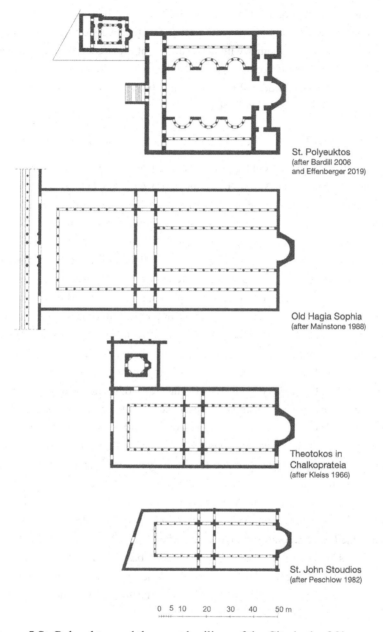

St. Polyeuktos
(after Bardill 2006
and Effenberger 2019)

Old Hagia Sophia
(after Mainstone 1988)

Theotokos in
Chalkoprateia
(after Kleiss 1966)

St. John Stoudios
(after Peschlow 1982)

0 5 10   20   30   40   50 m

Figure 5 St. Polyeuktos and the great basilicas of the City in the fifth century
(Credit: Drawing by D. Miznazi 2022)

up to the Middle Ages. The propylon of the Old Hagia Sophia is a final
important point of comparison, as it also contains images on the external
structure above the main entrance. The most significant difference between

the Church of St Polyeuktos and the fifth-century basilicas, however, is undoubtedly the ambitious architectural motif of the two-story *exedrae* in the *naos* (see Section 6) together with the extravagant architectural sculpture (see Section 7). While the decorative system of the early basilicas still was closely linked to the classical orders of Roman architecture, this centuries-old tradition ended with a flourish in St. Polyeuktos.

The Innovative Architecture of the City in the Sixth Century

Chronologically, St Polyeuktos was succeeded by Justinian's well-preserved churches of Sts. Sergius and Bacchus and Hagia Sophia, today's Küçük Ayasofya Camii and Ayasofya Camii respectively. These buildings provide dramatic testimony of the vibrance of Constantinople as an architectural laboratory and have often been consulted to explain the forms of St. Polyeuktos.[72]

Since one of the most striking features of St. Polyeuktos is the two rows of *exedrae* on both sides of the *naos*, the Church of St. Mary in Blachernai could, at least according to older reconstruction proposals, serve as an additional point of comparison. The appearance of this most important pilgrimage shrine of the Theotokos at Constantinople is roughly known to us by textual descriptions, since the monument itself has not been preserved.[73] A predecessor was rebuilt in the reign of Justin I (518–527), making it approximately contemporary with St. Polyeuktos. Procopius describes it as a three-aisled basilica with galleries and two rows of columns set in straight lines, except in the center (τὰ μέσα), where they recede (ὑποστέλλονται).[74] This has led some scholars like Cyril Mango to propose a reconstruction of *exedrae* within the nave's colonnades, which would have been an interesting parallel to St. Polyeuktos.[75] However, the term ὑποστέλλονται is used elsewhere by Procopius and exclusively in his description of the layout of an apse. It is therefore more likely that Procopius describes the perspective when looking into the church from the western entrance. In this way, the assumed *exedra* could form the apse of the church.[76] St. Mary in Blachernai should thus be thought of as a large, but standard, basilica, possibly with decorative columns in the apse.[77] Nevertheless, the building most importantly reminds us that despite the innovative features of Justinianic architecture, the basilica was still the most common type of church building.

---

[72] Ćurčić, "Design and Structural Innovation."

[73] *De aedificiis* I.3.3–5; *Anthologia Palatina* I.3; *De Ceremoniis* I.27; Mercati, "Due nove memorie," 28; Mango, *Art of the Byzantine Empire*, 125n14; Mango, "Origins of the Blachernae Shrine," 62n7.

[74] *De aedificiis* I.3.3–5; καὶ τὰ μὲν ἄλλα τοῦ νεὼ μέρη κατ᾿ εὐθὺ ἑστᾶσιν οἱ κίονες, κατὰ δὲ τὰ μέσα ὑποστέλλονται εἴσο. Mango, "Origins of the Blachernae Shrine," 64.

[75] Mango, "Origins of the Blachernae Shrine," 76, fig. 1; Tantsis, "So-called 'Athonite' Type," 7, fig. 5.

[76] I owe the understanding of this passage to Elodie Turquois and Marlena Whiting.

[77] Ousterhout, *Eastern Medieval Architecture*, 107.

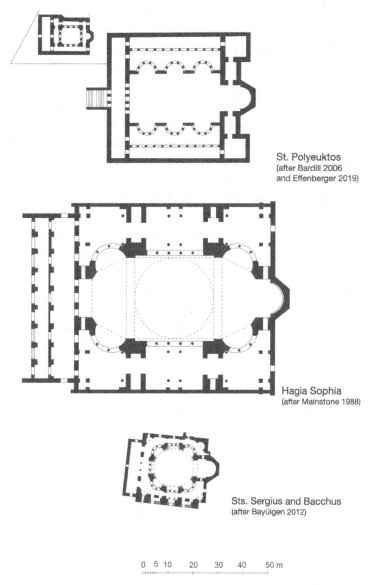

St. Polyeuktos
(after Bardill 2006
and Effenberger 2019)

Hagia Sophia
(after Mainstone 1988)

Sts. Sergius and Bacchus
(after Bayülgen 2012)

0 5 10   20   30   40   50 m

Figure 6 St. Polyeuktos and the great churches of Justinian in City in the sixth century (Credit: Drawing by D. Miznazi 2022)

The Church of Sts. Sergius and Bacchus represents one of Byzantium's most innovative architectural creations of early Byzantine architecture (Figure 6).[78] The plan includes a domed, octagonal core within an irregular rectangle. Piers

---

[78] Van Millingen, *Byzantine Churches*, 62–83; Ousterhout, *Eastern Medieval Architecture*, 186–189; Stroth, *Monogrammkapitelle*, 65–94.

define the octagonal *naos* of the church, but the space between them expands with alternating rectangular and curved recesses on two levels. In the interior, two columns each support an architrave between the dome piers, the course of which describes alternating shallow rectangular niches in the main axes and semicircular *exedrae* in the diagonals. This division of the walls on the ground floor is continued in the galleries, where the conches and niches are covered by arches that lead to a central pumpkin dome. The architrave between the second floor and the galleries bears an epigram of the founder, often mistakenly interpreted as an imperial reply to the text in St. Polyeuktos (see Section 6 and Figure 18).[79] While the open column positions conceal the basic shape of the octagon, it is the architrave that reveals the complicated basic shape of the complex interior (Figure 6).

Sts. Sergius and Bacchus and St. Polyeuktos can be meaningfully compared to one other. Both were richly decorated and displayed dedicatory epigrams surrounding the nave, combined with monograms on other parts of the sculpture (see Section 7). Both churches share the motif of *exedrae* over two stories as a distinctive feature of the internal arrangement (Figure 7). However, while innovative in terms of architectural layout, even Sts. Sergius and Bacchus shows some conservative features; instead of arches, the columns on the ground bear the "last architrave of antiquity" and the superposition of the orders of

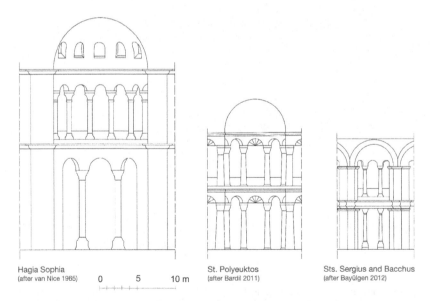

Hagia Sophia
(after van Nice 1965)   0   5   10 m

St. Polyeuktos
(after Bardil 2011)

Sts. Sergius and Bacchus
(after Bayülgen 2012)

Figure 7 The two-story exedrae of the sixth-century churches in Constantinople in comparison (Credit: Drawing by D. Miznazi 2022)

---

[79] Stroth, *Monogrammkapitelle*, 91–92.

capitals in the interior was justifiably recognized as a conservative element, which is completely left behind in the Hagia Sophia.[80]

When it comes to the architectural motif of two-story exedrae, reference must also be made to the church of St. John in Hebdomon.[81] The church's design finds its closest comparisons in the church of Sts. Sergius and Bacchus and San Vitale in Ravenna.[82] In addition, an inlayed column was found during the excavations, very similar to the architectural decoration of St. Polyeuktos (see Section 7).

Justinian's Hagia Sophia, then, is the best known and most influential of all Byzantine churches (Figure 6).[83] It has been considered the most important reference for our understanding of St. Polyeuktos, ever since the moment of the latter's discovery. Once the Old Hagia Sophia of emperor Theodosius II (see discussion earlier) had been burned in the Nika riots, the already existing plans for Hagia Sophia could be realized. After less than six years – in a remarkably short time – the new church was consecrated in 537 CE. It served as the cathedral of Constantinople and the setting for important imperial ceremonies, but it remained primarily a symbol of Justinian's dominion.

From an architectural point of view, Justinian's Hagia Sophia was an experiment on the grandest of scales.[84] The layout is often characterized as the juxtaposition of a longitudinal and centralized plan.[85] However, the innovative design of the Hagia Sophia cannot be explained in terms of its ground plan.[86] The only way to describe its form and concept adequately is by starting from the central motif of the dome. In fact, the floor plan of the *naos* should be considered only the result and projection of the dome's construction. In short, the structure was bricked from the bottom up, but designed from the top down. The search for buildings that anticipate the Hagia Sophia is futile, since both the design and the size of the Great Church have no predecessor and no immediate successor.[87]

When compared to St. Polyeuktos, the interior design of Sts. Sergius and Bacchus and Hagia Sophia shares the concept of sophisticated major spaces in the center with lateral rooms that are independent secondary structures (Figure 6). There is no total design for this group of churches, but the intention to create interiors of exceptional shape. This may also explain the emphasis on vertical axes by using the motif of two-story *exedrae* (Figure 7).

[80] Strube, *Polyeuktos und Hagia Sophia*, p. 91.
[81] Demangel, *Contribution*, 17–32; Kleiss, "Kirche des Täufers."
[82] Mathews, *Early Churches*, 55–61.
[83] For a comprehensive bibliography on Hagia Sophia see: Stroth, *Monogrammkapitelle*, 138–183
[84] Ousterhout, *Eastern Medieval Architecture*, 199.
[85] Ibid., 175. 199–216; Marinis, "Church Building," 183–185.
[86] Restle, "Konstantinopel," 428–434.
[87] Bogdanović, "Framing of Sacred Space," 251–252; Ousterhout, *Eastern Medieval Architecture*, 199; Marinis, "Church Building," 183–185.

In combination with the adventurous and ostentatious decoration, the rows of two-story exedrae created a completely new internal space for the church architecture of the City. The side aisles clearly become secondary structures in St. Polyeuktos, which no longer could be meaningfully connected to the naos. At the same time, St. Polyeuktos ended up being a conservative building that looked backward rather than forward. Robert Ousterhout was right to point out that the innovative designs of Justinianic architecture stand out both for their vaults and for the subtle geometric complexities that conceptually went far beyond those of St. Polyeuktos.[88] In fact, the exedrae of St. Polyeuktos were merely decorative and not integrated into the structural system in any meaningful way (Figure 6). Therefore, we certainly cannot ascribe to St. Polyeuktos a role as a prototype for Justinianic domed buildings, as has long been postulated.

4 The Dating

Early research quickly used historical data to establish an initial time frame of about fifteen years within which the church must have been constructed.[89] The epigrams do not mention Juliana's husband Areobindus, which suggests that he must have already been dead; hence, the church must have been built later then 512.[90] The death of the foundress Anicia Juliana, in turn, gives a *terminus ante quem* in 528. The aforementioned anecdote by Gregory of Tour relates a meeting of Juliana with Justinian, as emperor, and explicitly refers to Juliana as an old lady (see Section 2). For a long time, scholars used this anecdote as evidence to place the construction of the church at the end of the established time frame, namely, between 525 and 527.[91]

Brickstamps play a crucial role in the dating of the church of St. Polyeuktos, and the site has one of the most carefully studied collections of these artifacts. As in old Rome, the brickyards of Byzantium used to stamp half of the bricks they produced. These stamps sometimes allow us to determine both the place of origin and the production year of a batch of bricks.[92] Stephen Hill dated the stamps to 518–526, based on the observation that the church must have been completed by 527. Martin Harrison constrained this estimation to two clusters of brick, dating to 518–520 and 524–526. A reevaluation and redating of the material by Jonathan Bardill has challenged this chronological framework.[93] Following Bardill, the bricks from the substructure of St. Polyeuktos date to the period 508/9 to 511/22

---

[88] Ousterhout, "Aesthetics and Aesthetics and Politics," p. 104n4; Ousterhout, *Eastern Medieval Architecture*, 189.

[89] Mango and Ševčenko, "Remains," 244–245.   [90] Mango and Ševčenko, "Remains," 1961.

[91] Harrison, "The Church," 207–223.   [92] Ousterhout, "Review," 575.

[93] Bardill, *Brickstamps*; Reviews by Ousterhout, "Review," 575–577, and Sodini, "Remarques," 225–232, esp. 226–228.

and those of the superstructure to 517/18 to 521/22.[94] Whether the chronological gap between these two batches of bricks can be explained by an interruption of the work or rather by the use of older, stockpiled material in the substructures remains open to discussion. All that is certain is that the main body of the church was built sometime after September 1, 517. This would place the building into a rather different political sphere than the often-told story of challenging Justinian's authority whose coronation as emperor would not occur until ten years later in 527 (see Section 2).[95]

5 The Site

The spectacular circumstances of its rediscovery, the splendid architectural sculpture, and the extraordinary object itineraries of individual components of the church of St. Polyeuktos prompted scholars to have great expectations for the excavation work. However, the results have, at times, been considered disappointing.[96] In fact, only the substructures remain of what was once the largest and most lavishly decorated church in Constantinople. Not a single brick of the walls above the church's main body remain in situ.[97] Nevertheless, what excavations have yielded are still some of the most spectacular finds in Byzantine archaeology.

Topography

The church of St. Polyeuktos and the adjacent palace of Juliana were located in a central area of imperial property, especially the palaces of the Theodosian empresses, which extended along the Mese roughly between Philadelphion and the Forum of Markian (Figures 8 and 9). As indicated by the acute-angled formation of the southwest corner of the side church, the western boundary of the forecourt apparently followed the alignment of a road running along in a southwest-northeast axis and passing through the aqueduct of Valentinian. A main road running from the Charisios Gate (Sulukulekapı) across the Markian Forum into the City passed either the north or south side of the church.[98]

The Atrium and the Western Façade

The entire complex of St. Polyeuktos was about 100 meters long and 50 meters wide and accessible from the West through an atrium (Figure 9).[99] The course of

---

[94] Bardill, *Brickstamps*, pp. 62–64, pp. 111–116; Bardill, "A New Temple," 340.

[95] Ousterhout, "Review," 575; Ousterhout, "New Temples and New Solomons," 245–246.

[96] Peschlow, "Review," 628; Mango in Parpulov – Schachner 2010, 5.

[97] Harrison, *Excavations, vol. 1*, p. 20; Peschlow, "Review," 628.

[98] Effenberger, "Sasanidischer Baudekor", 159.   [99] Harrison, "The Church," 26–27.

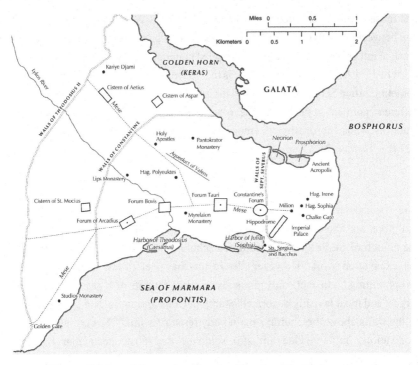

Figure 8 Map of Byzantine Constantinople with the location of
St. Polyeuktos in about the center of the peninsula (Credit: Map by C. Connor
and T. Elliott 2003)

Figure 9 Reconstructed view across the cityscape of Byzantine Constantinople.
The monumental building in the background on the left is St. Polyeuktos
(Credit: www.byzantium1200.com)

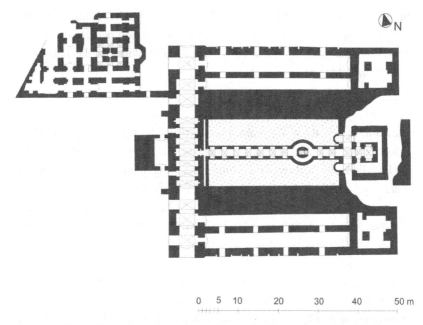

Figure 10 Simplified plan of the foundations of St. Polyeuktos (Credit: Drawing by D. Miznazi 2022 after Harrison 1989, Fig. 48)

an older road leads to an angled western end for this courtyard (Figure 10). Older research has assumed a *propylon* as the central gateway to the area, roughly similar to that which we know existed for the western entrance of the Old Hagia Sophia.[100] It has also been suggested on the basis of a medieval account that the atrium of St. Polyeuktos could have been open to the road.[101] Porticoes, which normally frame the interior of the courtyards of Christian basilicas, do not seem to have existed here. An outbuilding overlooked the northern third of the atrium (see discussion later).[102]

The western façade of the church is a special case for several reasons. The church building itself sat on a monumental platform in such a way that the floor level of the church rose 5 meters above the marble pavement of the atrium (see later). A large flight of steps bridged this difference in level and led to the three main portals. Remains of this nine-meter-wide staircase were still found during the excavations. We know from textual sources that large plaques with inscriptions were placed next to the portals of the western façade (see Section 6) and that three mosaic paintings with scenes from the life of Constantine the Great

---

[100] Harrison, "The Church," 412n28.

[101] Speck, "Juliana Anicia," 143–146; Effenberger, "'Sasanidischer' Baudekor," 158–159.

[102] Harrison, *Excavations, vol. 1*, pp. 24–26.

hung above them. All these features – the elevated church, the flight of steps leading to the elevated main entrance, and the inscription panels and mosaic paintings on the exterior – are very exceptional features in the history of Byzantine architecture.[103]

The Outbuilding

In the northern part of St. Polyeuktos' atrium lie the foundations of a building that look like a second, but much smaller, church. Even though this building stood literally in the shadow of the main church, it has barely been studied so far (Figure 10).[104] Scholars have tentatively identified it as the baptistery of St. Polyeuktos; other options include a palace building or even the burial chapel of the foundress Anicia Juliana.[105] In any case, the cross-vaulted grille foundations indicate that sophisticated and ambitious architecture must have existed above it as well.

A striking feature of its substructures is a central room (6 x 7 m) surrounded by a system of longitudinal and transversal foundation walls that form four lateral corridors around it, with two additional corridors to the west and a polygonal apse in the east. A key to understanding this architecture may lie in the middle of this central room: a strange square foundation of 4 x 4 meters (Figure 10). Four brick pillars in the corners of this foundation supported the brick vault of the central room, a barrel vault on each side, and a cross vault in each corner. In the center of the foundation was a cylindrical recess ($\emptyset$ 80 cm), which the inner sides of the brick piers accommodated with their carefully designed curves. The function of this recess remains a riddle. The excavator explained the foundation as the substructure of a *piscina* and reconstructed the building above as a baptistery.

This interpretation has at least two problems. The grille foundations of this complex suggest the existence of an elongated church building, but the early Byzantine baptisteries in Constantinople, as far as we know, tended to be centralized structures.[106] The baptisteries of St. Mary of Chalkoprateia and Hagia Sophia were octagonal central rooms with diagonal niches inscribed in an externally square building.[107] The substructures of the baptistery of St. Mary

---

[103] So far, only one attempt has been made to reconstruct this Western façade. Effenberger, "'Sasanidischer' Baudekor," 166, fig. 7.

[104] Harrison, *Excavations, vol. 1*, pp. 24–26, pp. 411–412; Harrison, *A Temple*, p. 64; Ćurčić, "Design and Structural Innovation," 36; Effenberger, "'Sasanidischer'" Baudekor," 180–185.

[105] Mathews, *Early Churches*, 55; Harrison, *Excavations, vol. 1*, 24–26; Effenberger, "'Sasanidischer' Baudekor," 180–185.

[106] Brandt, "Understanding the Structures," 1593.

[107] The baptistery of Hagia Sophia: Eyice, "Le baptistère"; Castelfranchi, "L'edificio battesimale"; for the baptistery of Chalkoprateia see Kleiss, "Neue Befunde" 157–161; Kleiss, "Grabungen", 217–222.

of Chalkoprateia show a comparable central base construction as a support for the *piscina* (Figure 5).[108] The curious foundation in the basement of St. Polyeuktos would in principle be able to support the heavy weight of a *piscina* placed above it, but what purpose would the cylindrical cavity below have served? Moreover, the question arises why the palace church of Juliana should have had a baptistery at all.[109]

Later on, the substructures of the outbuilding were covered with waterproof plaster to function as cisterns (see Section 10).

The Main Body of the Church

The main body of the church sat on a monumental pedestal 5 meters above the level of the atrium. While the church itself is lost today, the excavations have uncovered most of its substructures. This structure had a length of about 59 meters and a width of about 52 meters. The layout of this basement is the only archaeological source for understanding the construction of the church above it.

On each side of the main staircase was a door leading from the atrium down a few steps to the sub-narthex in the basement of the church (Figure 11).[110] This sub-narthex was a considerable hall of 40 meters long and 5 meters wide with ceilings made as cross vaults (Figure 10). This gives us an approximate idea of the quality of the church's fabric and the size of the narthex above.

The basement below the naos and naves of the church was crossed by five vaulted corridors in a west–east axis, corresponding to the five aisles of the basilica. Below the side aisles of the church, these corridors carried barrel vaults and mainly had a structural, nondecorative function. The passage in the central axis instead formed a structural unit with the sub-narthex and was a comparably sophisticated architecture with cross vaults. To the east, this central aisle ended in a multi-chambered crypt directly under the altar of the church, another unique feature of St. Polyeuktos (Figure 12).[111]

The Crypt

The eastern end of the axial corridor leads into a transverse hall, from which there are three entrances to the crypt (Figures 10 and 13). A threshold found in situ suggests that these doors were lockable. The two side doors lead into a Π-shaped ambulatory, the floor of which was covered with bricks, while the central door led through a small antechamber into the central room, the floor and walls of which were decorated with marble. This central chamber was a rectangular room with a small eastern niche and larger rectangular niches on either side.

[108] Kleiss, "Neue Befunde," 157–161.   [109] Effenberger, "'Sasanidischer' Baudekor," 180.
[110] Harrison, *Excavations, vol. 1*, 22–24.   [111] Restle, "Krypta," 466.

Figure 11 View from the sub-narthex to its northern entrance door. In the background on the left, the main staircase remains can be seen next to the marble slab floor of the atrium (Credit: Saraçhane Excavation Archive, University of Oxford)

A rectangular marble slab in the middle of the floor probably marked the former location of an altar or place of worship. Opposite the side entrances to the crypt were small round niches, the function of which unfortunately remains completely unknown. The unusual size and design of the crypt suggest that the relics of the church patron – medieval sources speak of the head of St. Polyeuktos – were kept here and made accessible.

Apart from St. Polyeuktos, only small cruciform altar crypts are known to have existed in the City during the fifth/sixth centuries; these include the Basilika of St. John Studios, the Church of the Theotokos in Chalkoprateia, the Church of St. Agathonikos, and the Church of Sts. Sergius and Bacchus.[112] The only evidence of a larger crypt in early Byzantine Constantinople is known to exist for the Church of St. John in Hebdomon.[113] Unfortunately, very few remains of the latter church building have been found. However, under the apse, two passages of 2.50 meters in height and 1.5 meters in width were unearthed.

---

[112] Mathews, *Early Churches*, p. 27, Fig. 10; Müller-Wiener, "Hagios Agathonikos?," 13.
[113] Demangel, *Contribution*, p. 19; Restle, "Krypta," 466.

Figure 12 View into the axial corridor looking east with numerous fallen marble pieces (Credit: Saraçhane Excavation Archive, University of Oxford)

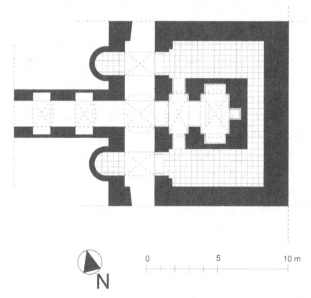

Figure 13 Plan of the crypt of St. Polyeuktos (Credit: Drawing by D. Miznazi 2022 after excavation sketchbook of G. Lawson)

In this case, the excavators believed to have found the entrances to a large crypt below the altar of the church.[114]

In St. Polyeuktos, the central corridor leading to the crypt was closed off at a later date.[115] Both accesses in the west and in the east show careful bricking. The exact date of this bricking is unknown, but the quality of the masonry led the excavators to assume that it took place shortly after the construction of the church. Therefore, the Church of St. Polyeuktos testifies an unprecedented form for a crypt, but we can say only little about its actual function as a sacred space in the early Byzantine topography of the City.

The Naos

The most striking feature for the reconstruction of the naos are the two wide foundation strips that extend along the entire length of the building (Figure 10). What was the reason for these oversized massive foundations? While older research believed large pillars were placed here to support a supposed dome, Jonathan Bardill hypothesized that we must assume two rows of three exedras each on these foundation strips (see Section 8).

The church's interior was magnificently decorated with marble paneling and rich inlay work. Small fragments of these wall coverings have been recovered in large numbers. Among them were various colorful marbles, such as red porphyry from Egypt, green porphyry from the Peloponnese, yellow marble from Tunisia, green breccia from Thessaly, black-and-white speckled marble from the Pyrenees, and many other varieties.[116]

The debris of the church revealed an abundance of mosaic tesserae embedded in small fragments of plaster that had fallen from the apse and walls. The mosaics are mainly made of glass, occasionally marble, limestone, and terracotta. Of the figurative fragments that have been found, all but one come from the apse area. There is good stratigraphic evidence that this vault mosaic belongs to the construction period of the church. This mosaic is thus of particular interest from an art-historical point of view, as it is the only figurative vault mosaic of the sixth century that has been discovered in Constantinople and that we can prove by its material remains.

Only limited remains of liturgical furniture from St. Polyeuktos could be found during excavation. The *synthronon* – a semicircular tiered bench for the clergy in the apse – has not survived in the archaeological record, but can be reconstructed with certainty.[117] Several fragments of magnificent inlaid

---

[114] Mathews, *Early Churches*, p. 57.   [115] Harrison, *Temple for Byzantium*, p. 64, fig 63.
[116] Ibid. pp. 77–78.
[117] Harrison, *Excavations, vol. 1*, 126, fig. 167, 134, fig. 171; Bardill, "A New Temple," 363, fig. 2.

columns were found in the altar area, which is why scholars would like to recognize these pieces as the supports of the *ciborium*.[118] A high *templon*, which can also be reconstructed with certainty, may have consisted of the many components of plinths, posts, and screens found during the excavations. However, none of this evidence is conclusive.

The most extraordinary piece of liturgical furniture is certainly the *ambo* of the church of St. Polyeuktos or, rather, its unique two-story construction (Figure 14). Although only a few fragments were found during excavation that could have belonged to an *ambo*, an oval foundation in the axial passage allows a reliable reconstruction of the pulpit. The shape and enormous size of this foundation suggest a similar structure to that described in detail by Paul the Silentiary regarding the rebuilding of Justinian's Hagia Sophia in 563 AD.[119] The central element was formed by the classical components of a Byzantine *ambo*, which is an oval pedestal supported by columns, to be ascended by a flight of steps in the east and west. Around this central element, eight higher columns were placed in a circle, supporting an architrave. Following Paul's description, we can reconstruct man-sized barrier plates between this outer ring of columns. For Hagia Sophia, we know that this area was the designated place for a choir.[120] This function could similarly explain the peculiarity of the *ambo* in St. Polyeuktos. Its oval foundation in the underfloor passage shows a recess in the eastern part with steps. These steep stairs made it possible to enter and leave the screened area below the *ambo* unseen from the underground corridor. While Harrison, who was responsible for excavations, suggested that it was used to present relics from the crypt to the public, it is equally possible that it was an entrance for the choir, or merely a supply entrance. In any case, these cellar steps are an unparalleled feature of the liturgical furniture in St. Polyeuktos.

6 The Epigrams

While the *Anthologia Palatina* contains copies of the two epigrams displayed outside and inside the Church of St. Polyeuktos, the tenth-century manuscript's compiler arranged the texts contrary to their sequence in the building and merged them into one long poem (Figure 1).[121] Marginal notes in the

---

[118] Harrison, *Excavations, vol. 1*, 78.

[119] Bardill, "A New Temple," 363, fig. 2; Paulos Silentiarius, Ambo; For the reconstruction of the ambo see Xydis 1947.

[120] Paulos Silentiarios Ambo; On the choirs in the Hagia Sophia and their dramaturgical staging during the liturgy see Moran, "The Choir," 1–3; Pentcheva, *Hagia Sophia*, pp. 35–38.

[121] Harrison, *Excavations, vol. I*, pp. 7–8; Speck, "Juliana Anicia," 133–147; Agosti and Gonelli, "La storia dell'esametro"; Connor, "Epigram in the Church," 496; Whitby, "The St. Polyeuktos Epigram," 595.

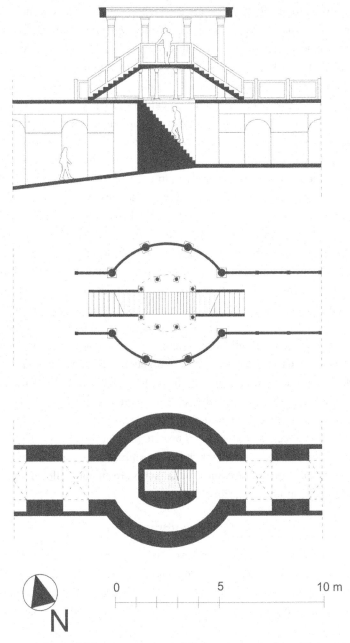

Figure 14 Reconstruction of the two-story ambo of St.
Polyeuktos (Credit: Drawing by D. Miznazi 2022 after excavation
sketchbook of G. Lawson)

manuscript provide relatively precise information regarding the placement of the epigrams. We know that verses 1–41 were placed in the *naos* of the church, while verses 42–73 were already visible in the atrium. These references to the spatial separation of the two epigrams correspond both with the archaeological findings and with inner-textual observations.[122]

The Ekphrasis at the Western Façade

The first epigram under discussion consists of an ekphrasis – a poetical description of a visual experience. Since no material remains of this inscription survive, it is not easy to reconstruct the specific materiality of this epigram. Instead, we have to rely solely on the information provided in the manuscript. A marginal note in the manuscript locates the text "at the entrance of the same church" (ἐν τῇ εἰσόδῳ τοῦ αὐτοῦ ναοῦ), while another writer's hand specifies its position "outside the narthex" (ἔξωθεν τοῦ νάρθηκος), that is, the western façade of the church. The manuscript also offers precise information about the arrangement and mise-en-page of the poem: "There are four panels on which this is written, five or six verses on each" (τέσσαρες εἰσὶ πίνακες ἐν ᾧ ταῦτα καὶ περιγράφονται ἀνὰ στίχους πέντε ἤ καὶ ἕξ). A final *scholion* next to verse 66 says: "This is the last panel, on the right side of the entrance, on which this is written" (ἔσχατός ἐστι πίναξ ὁ πρός τοῖς δεξιοῖς μέρεσι τῆς εἰσόδου ἐν ᾧ ἐπιγέγραπται τοῦτα).[123]

> What choir is sufficient to sing the work of Juliana who, after Constantine, embellisher of his Rome, after the holy golden light of Theodosius, (45) and after the royal descent from so many forebears, accomplished a work worthy of her family, and more than worthy?
>
> In a few years, she alone has overpowered time and surpassed the wisdom of the celebrated Solomon, raising a temple to receive God, the richly wrought and gracious splendor of which a great epoch cannot celebrate.

These first two panels (41–49) start with heavily embellished passages that invoke Anicia Juliana's illustrious predecessors in the building of great constructions. First, she links her name with her own famous family members and ancestors, including Constantine I and Theodosius II. The former was the founder of the City, which was then named after him; the latter was the founder of the largest church in *Constantinopolis* until the construction of St. Polyeuktos, Old Hagia Sophia (see Section 3). A reference to Solomon – a common topos of panegyric texts in Late Antiquity – also links her building project implicitly to the Temple of the Old Testament king (see Section 9).

---

[122] Sherry, *Hexameter Paraphrase*, p. 70; Whitby, "The St. Polyeuktos Epigram," 173–174.

[123] In addition, an abbreviated reference is given to one or more arches (πρὸς τ[ὴν] ἁψῖδ[α]), which has led to all sorts of speculations in research. Connor, "Epigram in the Church," 492–493.

(51) How it stands forth on deep-rooted foundations, springing up from below and pursuing the stars of heaven, and how too it extends from the west, stretching to the east, glittering with the indescribable brightness of the sun (55) on this side and on that! On either side of the central nave, columns standing upon sturdy columns

support the rays of the golden-roofed covering. On both sides recess hollowed out in arches, have given birth to the ever-revolving light of the moon. (60) The walls, opposite each other in measureless path, have put on marvelous meadows of marble,

Which nature caused to flower in the very depths of the rock, concealing their brightness and guarding Juliana's gift for the halls of God, so that she might accomplish divine works, (65) laboring at these things in the immaculate promptings of the heart. What singer of wisdom, moving swiftly on the breath of the west wind and trusting in a hundred eyes, will pinpoint on each side the manifold counsels of art, seeing the shining house, one ambulatory upon another? (70) Thence, it is possible to see above the rim of the hall a great marvel of sacred depiction, the wise Constantine, how escaping the idols he overcame the God-fighting fury, and found the light of the Trinity by purifying his limbs in water. Such is the contest that Juliana, after a countless swarm of labors, accomplished for the souls of her ancestors, and for her own life, and for those who are to come and those that already are.

These three panels (50–71) bear an ekphrasis of the church laced with symbolic language, connotations, and images. Although an ekphrasis cannot be expected to describe a building in art-historical terms, it – together with further support from excavation results – can help us determine some characteristics of its construction.[124] For example, we know that there were galleries on either side of the nave, and that supports resting on them held up the roof. The epigram's phrase referring to the ceiling (χρυσορόφου ἀκτῖνας ἀερτάζουσι καλύπτρης) was for a long time understood as clear evidence for a central dome, but the passage seems to refer instead to the gilded wooden beams or cassettes of a gable roof (see Section 8). *Exedrae* – or recesses hollowed out in arches – appear on both sides of the *naos*, which must refer to the galleries discussed above. The epigram's metaphor of these recesses "giving birth to the ever-revolving light of the moon" should be interpreted as evidence for possible windows – either in the calottes themselves, as is the case in the Hagia Sophia, or more likely in the clerestory running above them.[125] Other metaphors indicate that the walls were lined with precious marbles.[126]

---

[124] Mango and Ševčenko, "Remains of the Church," 245; Connor, "Epigram in the Church," 489–493; Whitby "The St. Polyeuktos Epigram'"

[125] See Friedländer 1912, 59n5 (Chorikios in Marc. II, 118).

[126] Wolf, "Marble Metamorphosis," 21.

The epigram concludes with a brief, but important, reference to three large images – likely executed in mosaic – which were presumably mounted above the portals of the church's western façade. They depicted episodes from the life of Constantine I: namely, the Battle of the Milvian Bridge, the Baptism of Constantine, and an additional battle scene.[127] We know little about pictorial decoration on the exteriors of early Byzantine churches, but the lunette image of Old Hagia Sophia may serve as a comparison (see Section 3).

Scholars have pointed out that there is a considerable discrepancy between the distribution of verses on inscription tablets given in the *Anthologia Palatina* and the syntax of the poem itself. Asterisks in the margins of the manuscript indicate five divisions of the epigrams into units of four, five, and six lines. Since this division of the poem resulted in broken phrases, it appeared problematic from a philological point of view. As a result, several scholars doubted the medieval entries in the *Anthologia*. Like Stadtmüller before him, Cyril Mango divided the text into six panels, which he would like to imagine in the form of monumental inscriptions placed along the entire length of the western façade.[128] Carolyn Connor suggested a regrouping of the relevant lines into "four grammatical divisions," found in the middle of line 47 and at the ends of lines 52, 59, and 65.[129] This idea has received much support, as it seems to solve the philological problems.[130] However, since no erroneous entries can be found in any other place within the *Anthologia Palatina*, it would be very surprising if, of all things, these later added details were incorrect.

The great Paul Friedländer had a more cautious view of the situation and suggested that the linguistic irregularities were perhaps rooted in the material design of the epigram.[131] Mary Whitby has also recognized strong grammatical breaks arising from the entries in the manuscript. However, instead of calling the medieval manuscript into doubt, she has arrived at a plausible solution to the problem by reconstructing the panels as being placed close together.[132] In this way, they could be "read as a continuous poem."[133] In fact, such a presentation of the plates would be more in accordance with the epigraphic habit of the time than all other scholarly hypotheses, which assume a spatial separation of the plates (Figure 15). This may also vindicate Paul Speck's disputed reflections on this epigram, which had argued for a reconstruction in which all five inscription panels were placed to the right of the main portal of the Church of St. Polyeuktos.[134]

---

[127] Milner, "Rightful Ruler," 79–80; Fowden, "Constantine, Silvester, and the Church," 153–168; Effenberger, "'Sasanidischer' Baudekor," 163–164.

[128] Stadtmüller 1894; Mango, "Notes d'épigraphie," 346–347.

[129] Connor, "Epigram in the Church," 495.   [130] Effenberger, "Sasanidischer' Baudekor," 162.

[131] Friedländer 1912, 59.   [132] Whitby, "The St. Polyeuktos Epigram," 161.   [133] Ibid.

[134] Speck, "Juliana Anicia," 137–138.

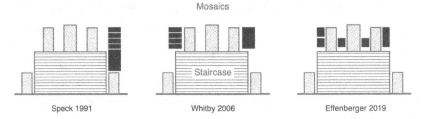

Figure 15 Proposals for the arrangement of the inscription panels on the western façade of St. Polyeuktos (Credit: Drawing by F. Stroth 2022)

Based on our previous discussion and from an archaeological perspective, we can conclude the following about the materiality of the epigram on the western façade of the Church of St. Polyeuktos. A visitor entering the atrium was confronted with an epigram inscribed on multiple panels. The very fact that this epigram was placed on panels (πίνακες) mounted on the outer wall is already exceptional for the early Byzantine period; we know other rare examples of large inscription panels from in San Vitale and San Apollinare in Classe in Ravenna.[135] Admittedly, they are from interiors; the outdoor inscriptions on San Vitale were executed as mosaics.[136] The letters of the St. Polyeuktos panels were undoubtedly executed as majuscules and arranged in *scriptio continua*, that is, written without spacing between the words, as was common for epigrams of that time. The inscription panels were probably made of marble, and polychrome highlighting of the text is very plausible. However, the size of the inscription panels and their exact locations around the portals remain unknown.

The Enkomion in the Naos

The state of our knowledge about the epigram in the interior of the church is substantially different since, during the excavation work, seven large-format marble blocks with fragments of this epigram were recovered.[137] These finds transformed our entire understanding of Byzantine epigram culture. Both the length of the epigram – the complete text is also preserved in the *Anthologia Palatina* – and the literary style of the text, as well as the idiosyncratic and magnificent elaboration of the carved letters in marble, are without comparison (Figures 2 and 16). The material reconstruction of the epigram becomes the source code for reconstructing the entire building. The highly fragmented components provide astonishingly far-reaching insights into the internal

---

[135] Nauerth, *Agnellus*, 320–321.   [136] Ibid. 280–281.
[137] Mango and Ševčenko, "Remains of the Church"; Harrison, *Excavations, vol. I*, pp. 117–119, Kat. 1a I – 1a vii.

Figure 16 Fragments of Great Entablature from St. Polyeuktos with verse 30 and the broken protome of a peacock (Credit: David Hendrix 2017; Saraçhane Excavation Archive, University of Oxford)

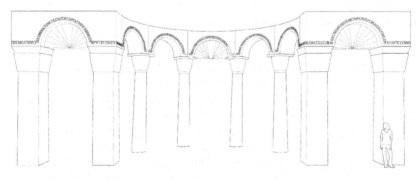

Figure 17 Schematic reconstruction of the central exedra in the northern aisle to show the size relationship of the epigram and the viewer (Credit: Stroth, *Monogrammkapitelle*, plate 120 c)

structure of the building (Figure 17).[138] The specific form of the text carrier allows a reliable reconstruction of the relevant parts, and, since we know the complete poem, a topology of the text in the different zones of the church can be traced at least partially (see Section 8).[139]

---

[138] Harrison, *Temple for Byzantium*, p. 88.
[139] On the reconstruction of the *exedrae*, see Bardill, "A New Temple"; Kakko, *Gebälkstücke der frühbyzantinischen Hagios Polyeuktos*, pp. 18–113, especially pp. 100–107.

A *scholion* in the *Anthologia Palatina* informs us that verses 1–41 are "written in a circle in the *naos* [of the church]" (Ταῦτα μὲν ἐν τῷ ναῷ ἔνδοθεν κύκλῳ περιγράφονται).[140] The text of the ekphrasis in the atrium also informs us that a two-story column construction rose on both sides of the central aisle, the vaults of which spread in apses on both sides (κίονες ἀρρήκτοις ἐπὶ κίοσιν ἐστηῶτες, χρυσορόφου ἀκτῖνας ἀμφοτέρωθεν ἀερτάζουσι καλύπτρης κόλποι δ' ἀμφοτέρωθεν ἐπ' ἀψίδεσσι χυθέντες ἀειδίνητον, φέγγος ἀειδίνητον ἐμαιώσαντο σελήνης.).[141]

The *enkomion* in the *naos* of the church draws on traditional themes for imperial praise, as prescribed in Menander Rhetor's treatise on the *Basilikos Logos*. The lines inscribed inside the church along the south side of the nave (1–21) begin by celebrating Anicia Juliana's imperial ancestor, her great-grandmother Eudocia, wife of Theodosius II, who built the first Church of St. Polyeuktos. They go on to compliment Anicia Juliana on her illustrious imperial ancestry; Eudocia's daughter Eudoxia was married to Emperor Valentinian III, while Juliana's parents were Placidia and the western emperor Olybrius. This glittering genealogy generates the novel epithet πολυσκήπτρων or "many-sceptered." The poet goes on to celebrate Anicia Juliana's own achievements; her most outstanding virtue is her orthodox Christian piety which has prompted her program of church-building.

> The empress Eudocia, in her eagerness to honour God, was the first to build a temple to the divinely inspired Polyeuktos; but she did not make it like this or so large, not from any thrift or lack of resources – for what can a queen lack? – (5) but because she had a divine premonition that she would leave a family which would know how to provide a better embellishment. From this stock Juliana, bright light of blessed parents, sharing their royal blood in the fourth generation, did not cheat the hopes of the queen, who was mother of finest children, (10) but raised this building from its small original to its present size and form, increasing the glory of her many-sceptred ancestors. All that she completed she made more excellent than her parents, having the true faith of a Christ-loving purpose. For who has not heard of Juliana, that, heeding piety, she glorified even her parents by her finely-laboured works? (16) She alone by her righteous sweat has made a worthy house for the ever-living Polyeuktos. For indeed she always knew how to provide blameless gifts to all athletes of the heavenly King. (20) The whole earth, every city, cries out that she has made her parents more glorious by these better works.

The lines on the north side of the nave (22–41) elaborate on Juliana's worldwide fame and piety in a sequence of three rhetorical questions. Juliana's numerous pious works secure her from oblivion; even Juliana herself,

---

[140] *AP* 1.10, 41 (*Scholion*).   [141] *AP* 1.10, 56–59.

it is suggested, has lost count of the number of churches that she built through-out the world (30–32). After stressing once again Juliana's industrious ancestors (34), the next part of the poem elegantly concludes (35–41) by comparing Juliana's churches to an immortal family. Running through the themes of ancestry, the text exemplifies Juliana's outstanding virtue of piety emphasizing her building achievements and concludes with a prayer for longevity.

> For where is it not possible to see that Juliana has raised up a glorious temple to the saints? Where is it not possible to see signs of the pious hands of you alone? (25) What place was there which did not learn that your purpose is full of piety? The inhabitants of the whole world sing your labours, which are always remembered. For the works of piety are not hidden; oblivion dies not wipe out the contests of industrious virtue. (30) Even you do not know how many houses dedicated to God your hand has made; for you alone, I think, have built innumerable temples throughout the whole earth, always revering the servants of the heavenly God. Following on all the well-labouring foot-steps of her ancestors, (35) she fashioned her ever-living stock, always treading the whole path of piety. Wherefore may the servants of the heavenly King, to whom she gives gifts and for whom she built temples, protect her readily with her son and his daughter. (40) And may the unutterable glory of the family of excellent toils survive as long as the Sun drives his fiery chariot.

The Epigram of Sts. Sergius and Bacchus. An Imperial Response?

In the Church of Sts. Sergius and Bacchus, a twelve-line epigram is carved in marble on the cornice surrounding the naos (Figure 18).[142] This epigram is often seen as an imperial response to the poems of St. Polyeuktos.[143] The numerous allusions to Anicia Juliana's glorious ancestry in the latter epigram should have provoked the imperial couple Justinian and Theodora to commission their own epigram. If this was indeed the case, then the much shorter epigram in the much smaller church would have been a very subdued reply on the imperial couple's part.

From an archaeological point of view, the two epigrams are comparable only to a limited extent and they are the result of very different concepts.[144] The poem of the Church of Sts. Sergius and Bacchus is an in situ work, composed specifically into the spatial frame of the octagon of this church. Only the

---

[142] It remains puzzling why the Anthologia Palatina does not contain the epigram of Sts. Sergius and Bacchus Church, although the text from the adjacent Peter and Paul Church is present (AP 1,8). See Stroth, *Monogrammkapitelle*, pp. 86–92.

[143] Connor, "Epigram in the Church," 511; Bardill, "The Church of Sts. Sergius and Bacchus," 4; Shahîd, "The Church of Sts. Sergios and Bakchos," 476–480; Croke, "Justinian, Theodora, and the Church," 50; Whitby, "The St. Polyeuktos Epigram"; Ousterhout, "New Temples and New Solomons," 247; Leatherbury, *Inscribing Faith*, p. 150; Talbot, "Patronage," 171; Viermann, "Surpassing Solomon," 224.

[144] Stroth, *Monogrammkapitelle*, pp. 81–94.

Figure 18 The epigram of Saints Sergius and Bacchus in Constantinople, today Küçük Ayasofya Camii in Istanbul (Credit: Sébah & Joaillier 1912)

deliberate arrangement of keywords within the text by the author of the poem enabled the stonemasons to chisel them out – the new titles of the imperial couple as *sceptered* Justinian and *god-crowned* Theodora – facing each other exactly in the lateral axis of the church. These keywords condense the central message of this dedicatory poem, and thus the literary and technical making of this epigram is inextricably linked. At the same time, the position of the keywords leads to a better understanding of the architecture, because only this alignment illustrates the significance of the transversal axis of the building.[145]

In the Church of St. Polyeuktos, the situation is completely different. Unlike in the latter church, the position of the individual verses or words does not seem to have played a role in the message of the epigram here. The decisive factor in this much longer poem was how the numerous verses could be transferred to the wall in a practicable and faultless manner. This was achieved by a one-verse-per-block system, that is, by always inscribing one line of the poem onto one marble component of the inscription frieze. Accordingly, the epigram was already carved on the ground before the blocks were installed, which is also indicated by the elaborate relief technique of the individual letters. In order to ensure a smooth workflow on a major construction site – as indeed St. Polyeuktos Church must have been – this system was one viable solution to actualize the epigram. The background of the inscription was painted blue, which made the text easy to read despite the high mounting.[146]

---

[145] Ibid. 93–94.

[146] Harrison, *Excavations, vol. 1*, p. 119, Kat. 1a vii. 414; Harrison, *Temple for Byzantium*, pp. 81–84; Fıratlı, *Sculpture byzantine figurée*, p. 213, Kat. 500 taf. 127.

Regarding the much discussed relationship between the visual (seeing) and discursive (reading) reception of Byzantine epigrams, we can assume that the carved letters inside St. Polyeuktos must have been clearly visible. However, the complex form of the church interior would have made it difficult to read the full text and not only because of its literary level. While common inscriptions on panels, like the ekphrasis on the western façade of the church, call for people to stop and read, the epigram inside St. Polyeuktos likely invited readers to move through the *naos* and "read with their bodies as well as with their eyes."[147] The epigrams on and in St. Polyeuktos can thus be described as part of a performative strategy for perceiving the building as a whole.

7 The Architectural Sculpture

The excavations at Saraçhane unearthed an abundance of decorative material, including various colored marbles, columns inlaid with glass and amethysts, and floor and wall mosaics. However, the prominent role of St. Polyeuktos in the history of Byzantine archaeology is based, above all, on its architectural sculpture, which has opened up a repertoire of motifs previously almost unknown, and its variety of forms is still difficult to position within the established narratives.[148] Indeed, its very existence sometimes seems a quiet embarrassment or even a negation of several of the field's traditional assumptions about the directions of cultural influence and Eurocentric concepts about the origins and functions of ornament and form.[149] This is well illustrated when the sculpture is labeled "exotic" by excavator Martin Harisson or when Cyril Mango calls the taste of Anicia Juliana "gaudy for a lady of ancient lineage."[150]

The architectural sculpture of St. Polyeuktos makes a strange impression on the classically trained viewer.[151] The decorated pieces often show two tendencies of ornamentation, which frequently appear on one and the same decorated piece and apparently aim at a deliberate contrast.[152] Therefore, ornamental motifs are divided into two main groups: one more traditional, although rarely classical, and one that shows almost unknown and unusual motifs in Byzantine art. The excavator Martin Harrison identified these two types of architectural decoration in the church and labeled them with the terms "classical" and "exotic." According to this, the classical group is based on the

---

[147] Leatherbury, *Inscribing Faith*, p. 149.

[148] Deichmann, "Pilastri acritani," 85; Harrison *Excavations, vol. 1*, pp. 414–418; Russo, "La Scultura di S. Polieucto"; Brands, "Persien und Byzanz," 245.

[149] Canepa, *The Two Eyes of the Earth*, p. 211.   [150] Mango, *Byzantine architecture*, p. 58.

[151] Deichmann, "Pilastri acritani," 85; Brands, "Persien und Byzanz," 245–251.

[152] Strube, *Polyeuktoskirche und Hagia Sophia*, pp. 61–75.

Figure 19 Cornice decorated with box-monograms between modillions and palmettes (Credit: Harrison, *Temple for Byzantium*, Fig. 103)

repertoire of Hellenistic-Roman art, the exotic group, by contrast, is explained by most researchers, following Harrison, in terms of the influence of Sasanian models.[153]

The most prominent examples of the "classical" group are the reliefs with grapevines on the Great Entablature block with the epigram (Figures 2, 16, and 22). For the veristic details, such as the vines and leaves, some of which overlap, they can indeed be compared to examples of Imperial Roman art. However, in the case of the other exponents of the "classical group," an orientation toward imperial-period models is not quite so obvious. While the ornamentation of the cornices (Figure 19), for instance, borrows many individual elements that were decisive for works of the imperial period, one can also recognize a strong effort to create a new formal language in these reliefs.

On the one hand, in the architectural ornaments of St. Polyeuktos, we find many motifs that undoubtedly derive from traditional Roman visual culture, such as grapevines, peacocks, and stylized acanthus leaves. These well-known motifs are intentionally altered and alienated by geometric elements. A reason for the novel impression left by this ornamentation is that both wall surfaces and structural elements are now covered with ornamentation to the same extent. This was radically new and is one of the reasons why the architectural sculpture of St. Polyeuktos – despite all its peculiarity – can be considered path-breaking for the further development of Byzantine visual culture. Friedrich Wilhelm Deichmann, at least for the column capitals, saw forerunners neither in the

---

[153] Grabar, *Sculptures byzantines de Constantinople*, pp. 59–65; Russo, "La scultura di S. Polieucto"; Ousterhout, *Eastern Medieval Architecture*, p. 184; Dodd, "Islamic States and the Middle East," 202.

Figure 20 Basket-capital on the excavation site (Credit: Saraçhane Excavation Archive, University of Oxford)

Figure 21 Pier capital (*pilastri acritani type*) on the excavation site (Credit: Deutsches Archäologisches Institut, D-DAI-IST-Inv-011643)

preceding Constantinople architectural sculpture nor elsewhere in Byzantine architecture (Figures 20 and 21).[154] On the other hand, Christine Strube has attempted to show that the capitals are very much the result of a process that goes back to the second century AD, and that the tradition of imperial Western Asia Minor architectural sculpture fed them substantially.[155]

[154] Deichmann, "Pilastri acritani," 85.
[155] Strube, *Polyeuktoskirche und Hagia Sophia*, pp. 75–77.

Figure 22 Corner-block of the Great Entablature with line 9 of the epigram and a pier capital on the excavation site (Credit: Saraçhane Excavation Archive, University of Oxford)

However, alongside these more traditional motifs, though in some respects unconventional, there is Harrison's "exotic group," which scholars almost unanimously proclaim to be influenced by Sasanian art. In fact, the Sasanian explanation is much older than one would suspect. Already in 1904, long before the rediscovery of the church in Istanbul, the influential art historian Josef Strzygowski wrote about the pilastri acritani (Figure 3) in Venice that:

> The woven of the smooth, massive surface with ornaments seems oriental [...]
> A parallel example [...] can be found in the Sassanid monuments.[156]

He claimed this primarily with the intention of giving Antioch a leading role in the "Orient or Rome" debate, a crucial art-historical controversy at the beginning of the twentieth century.[157] The Sasanian element is considered also to be present in the Great Entablature blocks with the epigram that was brought to light during excavations (Figure 22). Here the "classical" decorated sides of the marbles are contrasted with a decorative system in which vine leaves and grapes also appear, but now incorporated into a dominant geometric lattice network. Such geometric pattern systems based on rhombs, octagons, and circles are known especially for the stucco decoration of Sasanian architecture. The forms and motifs of many of the capitals of St. Polyeuktos also do not occur in Late Antique and Byzantine architecture and may also parallel Sasanian motifs (Figures 22 and 23).

---

[156] Strzygowski 1904, 433.   [157] Foletti and Lovino, *Orient oder Rom?*.

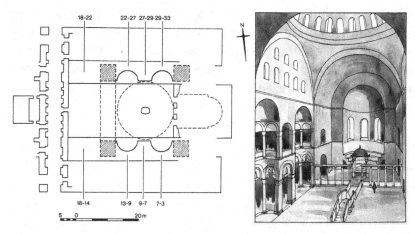

Figure 23 The Harrison reconstruction (Credit: Harrison, *Temple for Byzantium*, Fig. 167 and 169)

The mode by which these motifs entered the stonemasonry workshops of St. Polyeuktos is unclear, and there are several issues with the supposed models. Some small portions of the ornamental material may have parallels in Sasanian silk. However, Sasanian stuccowork and the architectural ornament at Taq-e Bostan in modern Iran provide the closest precursors for most of the material. There is a small school of German archaeologists who insist, with good reasons, on the methodological issues in this discussion, but in the end without offering more convincing explanations.[158] The main criticism is that all convincing parallels are dated contemporary or later than St. Polyeuktos, the forms of which one tries to explain by the references.

Another striking feature is the extensive use of monograms as an integral element of ornamentation (Figure 19).[159] This connects the architectural sculpture of St. Polyeuktos with the Justinianic churches of the City, such as the Church of Sts. Sergius and Bacchus, Hagia Eirene, and Hagia Sophia.[160] Unlike in the latter buildings, however, the monograms in St. Polyeuktos cannot be deciphered to this day; the name Anicia Juliana, for example, is not among them.[161] Only the monograms of the *Pilastri Acritani* (Figure 3) can be resolved as Ἁγίου Πολυεύκτου, as Martin Harrison suggested in a letter to Cyril Mango as early as 1965, but which he himself never published.[162]

---

[158] Strube, *Polyeuktoskirche und Hagia Sophia;* Brüx, *Zur sassanidischen Ornamentik;* Brands, "Persien und Byzanz."

[159] Harrison *Excavations, vol. 1*, plate 111–116; 118–120.

[160] Stroth, *Monogrammkapitelle*, pp. 111–113.

[161] Garpizanov, *Graphic Signs of Authority*, p. 163.

[162] Letter by Martin Harrison to Cyril Mango, February 2, 1965 (Saraçhane Excavation Archive, University of Oxford).

Perhaps even Mathew Canepa was still too optimistic when he stated that "the field of late Roman and Byzantine archaeology is only beginning to fully integrate the St. Polyeuktos sculptures into its narrative."[163] While the architectural sculpture of St. Polyeuktos is frequently being discussed and illustrated, we are still far from a full integration of these marbles into Byzantine art history.

8 The Reconstructions

Soon after its discovery, St. Polyeuktos was considered one of the most important exemplars of early Byzantine architectural history.[164] Despite its importance, hardly any scholarly discussion seems to have transpired about the reconstruction of the building. Other aspects, such as the outlandish architectural sculpture, its objects' itineraries (see Section 7), or the idea that the church was a copy of the Temple (see Section 9), seem to have completely absorbed scholarly attention. The reconstruction of the church with a central brick dome by the excavator, Martin Harrison, benefited from his authority and remained the accepted solution for decades.[165] Jonathan Bardill is known to be the first who raised the question again and proposed a new reconstruction of the building, now with a wooden pitched roof, as this would have been more common for Late Antique basilicas.[166] His proposal finds broad agreement today.[167] A closer look at the history of research and into the excavation archives reveals that the reconstruction of St. Polyeuktos has always been highly controversial and much more vividly discussed than commonly assumed. These early reviews and comments are of particular interest for us since they anticipated key aspects of the reconstruction proposal valid today.

History of Research

To properly frame the history of the reconstruction of St. Polyeuktos, we must first understand the situation of Byzantine architectural historiography in the mid-twentieth century, when the site was rediscovered. The origin of the central dome as the crowning achievement of Byzantine architecture had an irresistible attraction for architectural historians in those days.[168] Like "Kuppelbasilika" for an enthusiastic German school at the beginning of the century, the term "domed basilica" carried the same hypnotic quality in English.[169] Particularly popular was

---

[163] Canepa, *The Two Eyes of the Earth*, p. 211.

[164] Mango, *Architettura bizantina*, p. 98; Brenk, *Spätantike und frühes Christentum*, p. 88.

[165] Harrison, *Excavations, vol. 1*, pp. 406–418; Harrison, *A Temple for Byzantium*, pp. 127–134.

[166] Bardill, "A New Temple"; Bardill, "Église."

[167] Ousterhout, *Eastern Medieval Architecture*, pp. 182–184, fig. 8.11; Effenberger, "'Sasanidischer' Baudekor," 158.

[168] Harrison, *A Temple for Byzantium*, pp. 25–26.   [169] Strzygowski, *Kleinasien*, p. 51.

a discussion around a group of late-fifth-/sixth-century Cilician churches in Alahan, Meryemlık, Corykus, and Dağ Pazarı.[170] While the scholarly group of "dome hunters"[171] reconstructed these buildings with central vaults, others – and indeed most researchers today – rather hypothesize that these churches had tower-like constructions crowned by wooden pyramid roofs.[172] Both groups of scholars agreed to recognize these buildings as prototypes or at least important stages for the architectural innovations in sixth-century Constantinople.[173] The excavator of St. Polyeuktos Martin Harrison was actively involved in this discussion.[174] With the rediscovery of the church in Istanbul, a missing link in the evolution of Byzantine architecture seemed to be at hand.[175] To reconstruct this splendid church in the capital of the Byzantine Empire without a central dome was hardly thinkable for the academic community at the time.

The Harrison Reconstruction

What came to light during the excavations, however, provided ambiguous evidence concerning the superstructure of the church. Looking ahead to Hagia Sophia, excavator Harrison quickly suggested that a central dome would be appropriate in sixth-century Constantinople and therefore the most probable reconstruction for the roofing of St. Polyeuktos.[176] The 5-meter-high platform on which the church rests, as well as the enigmatic oversized foundation strips on either side of the naos, was explained as supports for massive pillars of a central dome.[177]

A plan of the church reconstructed in this way and complemented by a perspective drawing of the interior executed in watercolor shaped our understanding of this monument for quite a long time (Figure 23).[178] At one time, even the plan of Hagia Sophia was projected directly onto the founda-tions of St. Polyeuktos "to suggest some kind of superstructure that would fit."[179] Even the architects of Hagia Sophia were fitted into this hypothesis;

---

[170] For comprehensive studies see Hill, *The Early Byzantine Churches of Cilicia*.

[171] Hill, *The Early Byzantine Churches of Cilicia*, 45.

[172] Forsyth, "Architectural Notes," 223–236; Gough, "The Emperor Zeno," 236.

[173] Guyer and Herzfeld, *Meriamlik und Koykos*, pp. 61–62; Hill, *The Early Byzantine Churches of Cilicia*.

[174] Harrison, "Churches and Chapels"; Harrison, "Monastery of Mahres Dağ"; Harrison, "Inscriptions and Chronology"; Harrison, *A Temple for Byzantium*, pp. 25–28.

[175] Harrison, "Inscriptions and Chronology," 33.

[176] Harrison, "Excavations at Saraçhane," 83; Harrison, *Excavations, vol. 1*, p. 408.

[177] Harrison, *Excavations, vol. 1*, p. 406–411; Ibid. *A Temple for Byzantium*, 126–135; Brüx, "Zur sassanidischen Ornamentik," 6–7n27.

[178] Harrison, *A Temple for Byzantium*, p. 126, fig. 167; Mathews and Muller, *Dawn of Christian Art*, p. 180, fig. 6.17.

[179] Harrison, "Excavation Report," 548, Taf. 277, fig. 20; Compare also Krautheimer, "Response to Deichmann," 447.

Isidore of Miletus and Anthemius of Tralles were assumed to have built St. Polyeuktos as an early work.[180] However, Harrison always had to admit that nothing was found during the excavations that could be attributed to a dome.[181]

The Harrison Correspondence

For this reason, the excavator repeatedly consulted leading authorities in the field of Byzantine architecture for advice on reconstruction.[182] Respondents were less than enthusiastic about Harrison's attempt to reconstruct the building in the style of Hagia Sophia. The feedback was unanimously critical, sometimes in very clear terms. Robert van Nice, who was busy at the time with his epochal architectural survey of Hagia Sophia and to whom Harrison was jokingly "envious of a man who actually has a dome!"[183] was "quite clear that the form of St. Polyeuktos' foundations bears little or no relation to the form of those of St. Sophia."[184] The architectural historian Paul Underwood, then Dumbarton Oaks field director, has commented several times on Harrison's reports:

> While the theory that the church was an earlier version of the S. Sophia type was very tempting you are right to consider other possibilities, even probabilities. I shall wait patiently for your reasoning that leads you to an other interpretation of the superstructure.[185]

He also wrote a harsh peer review of Harrison's Fourth Preliminary Report of the excavation to be published in the *Dumbarton Oaks Papers* and added the sketch of his own reconstruction proposal (Figure 24):

> I am quite puzzled about how one could interpret the plan, as you drew it, in terms of elevation. I refer especially to your indications of reflected vaults on the plan. I cannot reconstruct the elevation at all in terms of your indicated vaults. I have sketched and enclose what I think is at least one possible interpretation, both in half plan and a superstructure and it is hardly satisfactory aesthetically in its proportions. I would suggest, Martin, that the reconstruction requires considerably more study and would therefore suggest that you do not publish it yet. Everything has gone off but it would be no trick at all, if you wished, to delete the plan and the paragraph referring to it when galleys are out. Sorry about this, and, <u>please</u>, don't be upset at my reaction.[186]

---

[180] Harrison and Fıratlı, "Second and Third Preliminary Reports," 229.
[181] Harrison, *Excavations, vol. 1*, pp. 408–409; Harrison, *"A Temple for Byzantium,"* p. 130.
[182] The correspondence is kept in the Saraçhane Excavation Archive, Oxford University.
[183] Letter by M. Harrison to R. van Nice, January 6, 1967, Saraçhane Excavation Archive.
[184] Ibid.
[185] Letter by P. Underwood to M. Harrison, July 17, 1967, Saraçhane Excavation Archive.
[186] Letter by P. Underwood to M. Harrison, October 19, 1967, Saraçhane Excavation Archive.

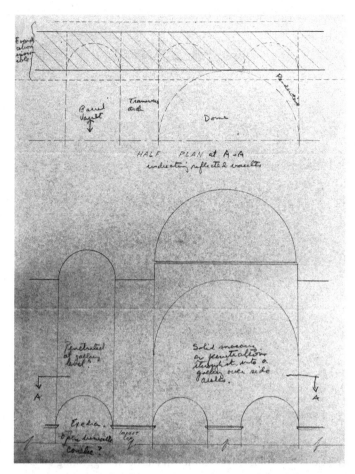

Figure 24 Letter by Paul Atkins Underwood to Martin Harrison suggesting reconstruction of St. Polyeuktos, October 19, 1967 (Credit: Saraçhane Excavation Archive, University of Oxford)

And so, the mentioned plan of the church was removed from Harrison's paper and unfortunately never printed.[187] In place of the original text, a critical passage was introduced which calls the reconstruction of the church "a complicated problem." It concludes by stating that "a central dome over the two eastern pairs of *exedrae* seems to be possible, but a basilical roofing cannot be entirely ruled out."[188]

John Hayes, who is best known for having published the pottery from the excavation, was also enthusiastically involved in the question of reconstruction.

---

[187] Harrison, "Excavations at Saraçhane," 1965.
[188] Harrison, "Excavations at Saraçhane," 1965, 276.

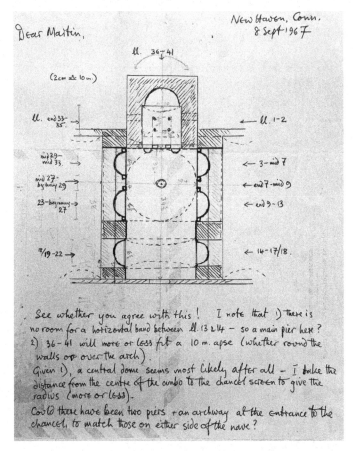

Figure 25 Letter by John Hayes to Martin Harrison suggesting an alternative reconstruction of St. Polyeuktos, September 8, 1967 (Credit: Saraçhane Excavation Archive, University of Oxford)

He sent several letters with sketches explaining his ideas, including his own proposal for the reconstruction of the church (Figure 25). He assumed three *exedrae* on both sides and was an early voice in pointing out that the internal epigram is not sufficiently considered during the process of reconstruction.[189]

The architectural historian Peter Megaw also had problems with Harrison's proposal:

> I am bothered by the lack of any reflection of a domical superstructure in the foundation plan. I believe it to be a general Byzantine practice to have foundations below dome arches, as well as on the cords of apses. On the other hand, in the Polyeuktos foundations, I see nothing to conflict with

---

[189] Letter by J. Hayes to M. Harrison, September 8, 1967, Saraçhane Excavation Archive.

a basilican superstructure. Equally, if your siting of the exedrae is correct, the basically uniform plan of the nave calls for an equally uniform superstructure. Your solution is awkward also in one point of detail: the heavy blocks of masonry carrying the dome arches would almost block the lateral openings of the exedra colonnades. Consequently, though I am happy about your arrangement of the exedrae, I would not like to underwrite your proposal for the superstructure at this stage.[190]

It may have been all of these objections that have driven Martin Harrison to not include a reconstructed floor plan of the church within the originally submitted manuscript of his final monograph, nor to add any sections or other reconstruction drawings of the building. The only reason any drawings can be found in the publication at all is due to the fact that the editor of Dumbarton Oaks – presumably Julia Warner or Paul Underwood himself – vehemently insisted on it.[191] Harrison later published the well-known reconstruction, but always remained somewhat uncertain about the solution he found. To Robert van Nice he wrote:

> There are difficulties in my proposal scheme. If this was an experimental centrally domed basilica, doubtless the architect(s) had headaches too![192]

Even after the publication of the final monograph, criticism of Harrison's proposal did not cease. Thomas F. Mathews pointed to the alternative possibility of wooden roof construction and, with explicit reference to relevant passages in Gregory of Tours, wrote that:

> Whether the galleries in turn sustained a brick dome or simply a timber roof cannot be securely decided on the basis of present evidence; both the inscription and the story of Gregory of Tours speak of a gilded ceiling in ambiguous terms that could refer either to vaulted or timber-roofed constructions.[193]

Cyril Mango was "not entirely happy with the proposed reconstruction"[194] and assumed "six instead of four exedrae which would produce a very different interior plan."[195] Urs Peschlow raised doubts about the reconstructed barrel vaults in the galleries.[196] Rowland Mainstone had general doubts about the

---

[190] Letter by P. Megaw to M. Harrison, November 15, 1967, Saraçhane Excavation Archive, University of Oxford.

[191] The schematic map of Constantinople (Harrison, *Excavations, vol. 1*, p. 4, fig. A) as well as the drawing of the monograms (Harrison, *Excavations, vol. 1*, p. 162, fig. L) are also only in the book due to the demands of the editor.

[192] Letter by M. Harrison to R. Van Nice, January 6, 1967, Saraçhane Excavation Archive, University of Oxford.

[193] Mathews, *Early Churches*, p. 53; see also Brüx, "Zur sassanidischen Ornamentik," 8.

[194] Mango, "Review of Harrison 1986 and 1989," 238.

[195] Mango, *Architettura bizantina*, p. 98; Mango, "Review of Harrison 1986 and 1989," 238.

[196] Peschlow, "Review of Harrison," 628.

reconstruction of a dome and instead advocated a tower-like structure with a wooden pyramid roof.[197]

> Martin Harrison's reconstruction of Hagios Polyeuctos as a more direct fore-runner of Hagia Sophia similarly fails to explore the full implications. The crucial relationship between the exedrae and the four main piers and the main lateral arches are simple ignored, and the near impossibility of reconciling these forms where they meet in the aisles seems to rule out this reconstruction.[198]

Almost all renowned Byzantine architectural experts of the time commented on Harrison's reconstruction of the building – and all these voices were critical. Unfortunately, this criticism never developed into a productive academic discussion. Thus, the Harrison reconstruction of St. Polyeuktos with a central dome remained without "official" alternatives for many decades.[199]

The Bardill Reconstruction

This situation only changed with the work of Jonathan Bardill and his ground-breaking reinterpretation of the building.[200] His breakthrough was also made possible by the fact that for the first time the epigram was taken seriously as the "source code" for questions of reconstruction. After a reevaluation of the archaeological and textual sources, Bardill finally confirmed the older doubts that the church of St. Polyeuktos did not have a central dome.[201] He redesigned the building as a five-naved basilica with "classical" wooden roofing; the central nave was covered with a saddle roof and the aisles with corresponding pent roofs.[202] The wide foundation strips were explained for the first time as substructures of tripartite rows of *exedrae* on the side of the naos, whereas the previously assumed arrangement of four large piers could never have been reconciled with the excavated structures (Figure 5).[203]

Bardill points to the Latin term *camera* used by Gregory of Tour to describe the roof of St. Polyeuktos can denote both vaulted and flat ceilings.[204]

---

[197] Mainstone, *Hagia Sophia*, 159–160; compare Connor, "Epigram in the Church," 515.

[198] Mainstone, "Structural Analysis," 339n38.

[199] Mango and Ševčenko, "Remains of the Church," 247; Deichmann, "Review Krautheimer," 117; Mango, *Architettura bizantina*, p. 98; Ćurčič, "Design and Structural Innovation," 23–24.

[200] Bardill, "A New Temple"; Bardill, "Église Saint-Polyeucte."

[201] Bardill, "A New Temple," 366; Bardill, "Église Saint-Polyeucte," 93–100; Early voices for wooden constructions have been Th. F. Mathews, R. Mainstone, and P. Megaw.

[202] Bardill, "A New Temple," 361, 363, fig. 2.

[203] Still for the reconstruction of a central dome: Russo, "Architettura e scultura," 75; Ders., "Introduzione ai capitelli," 129–131; Ćurčič, "Design and Structural Innovation," 189–191; McKenzie, *Architecture of Alexandria*, p. 334; Bogdanović, *Framing of Sacred Space*, p. 268 n20; Undecided: Engemann, *Römische Kunst*, p. 155.

[204] GM 102, p. 106, 15–19; Bardill, "A New Temple," 345–366; Already earlier, Deichmann, "Decke," 250–252 and Mathews, *Early Churches*, p. 53 have pointed out that.

The latter's text continues that Juliana should order her craftsmen to make panels (*tabulae*) of the right size for the roof (*iuxta mensuram tegnorum*), to fix them to the roof (*camerae adfixerunt*), and to cover them with gold (*texeruntque ex auro mundissimo*). Today this is interpreted to mean that the tie beams of the wooden roof construction of St. Polyeuktos were paneled with a gilded coffer ceiling. We have prominent comparisons for gilded paneling of the ceilings of Late Antique basilicas, such as the Lateran Basilica in Rome or the Church of the Holy Sepulchre in Jerusalem. But there is no compelling argument to interpret the gilded ceiling of St. Polyeuktos Church as an architectonic manifestation of Ezekiel's temple.[205]

In addition, the ekphrasis on the west façade of the building reports that the columns of the church "support the rays of the golden-roofed covering" (χρυσορόφου ἀκτῖνας ἀερτάζουσι καλύπτρης).[206] Older research was uncertain regarding whether it referred to the radiant ribs of a golden dome or simply the rays of light.[207] The written sources thus remain unspecific; ultimately, the archaeological findings tip the scales in favor of reconstructing St. Polyeuktos today with a pitched roof.

The Internal Arrangements: The Exedrae

The archaeological findings of two exedrae that faced each other on both sides of the Naos intertwine so closely and revealingly that their reconstruction is reliably possible (Figure 26).[208] Of the only seven fragments of the great entablature with rests of the epigram that became known during the excavations, as many as six blocks can be reliably assigned to these two semicircular

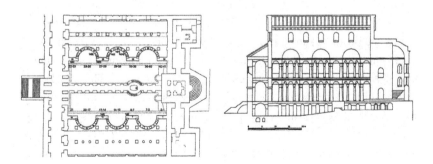

Figure 26 The Bardill reconstruction (Credit: Bardill, "Église Saint-Polyeucte," Figs. 4 and 6)

---

[205] Bardill, "A New Temple," 345–346. [206] *AP* 1.10.57.
[207] Harrison, *Excavations, vol. 1*, p. 408 with n. 10; Connor, "Epigram in the Church," 491.
[208] Bardill, "A New Temple," 360–365; Ibid., "Église Saint-Polyeucte," 88–91, fig. 5

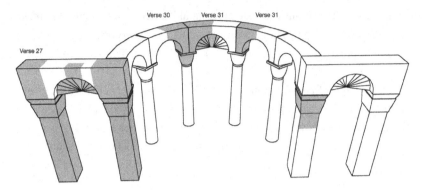

Figure 27 Simplified reconstruction of the northern exedra with all excavated parts marked in grey (Credit: Stroth, *Monogrammkapitelle*, plate 120b)

niches in the center of the church's interior.[209] Fortunately, the few preserved components come from critical key points of the construction (Figure 27). The reconstruction of the central exedrae discussed here differs in crucial points from that of Martin Harrison and Jonathan Bardill.[210]

The backbone for the reconstruction of the northern exedra is formed by three blocks of the great entablature, which are inscribed with the successive verses 30, 31, and 32 and thus undoubtedly become recognizable as belonging together (Figure 28).[211] The length and curvature of these blocks allow the exedra to be completed into a semicircle consisting of a total of five curved blocks, with one verse of the epigram carved on every block (Figure 17).[212] M. Harrison instead had reconstructed the exedrae with only three curved blocks, and J. Bardill has proposed a solution with three full blocks and two half blocks on the outer sides.[213] The crucial argument is to be found in the materiality of the epigrams, in how the poem became a physical part of the church. Each of the surviving blocks shows either the beginning of a verse on the left margin (Figure 2) or the end of a verse on the right margin (Figures 16 and 28). This block-wise distribution of the verses can be traced for all preserved structural elements of the two central exedrae in the described manner.[214] The only exception to this rule is a smaller fragment with remnants of verse 25/26.[215] This fragment thus comes from the western part of the northern row of exedrae. However, we have no other archaeological information about the exedrae placed there.

[209] Bardill, "A New Temple"; ibid., "Église Saint-Polyeucte"

[210] Harrison, *Excavations, vol. 1*, p. 407; Bardill, "Église Saint-Polyeucte," 88–91.

[211] Harrison, *Excavations, vol. 1*, p. 407.   [212] Kakko, *Gebälkstücke*, pp. 18–76.

[213] Harrison, *Excavations, vol. 1*, p. 409; Harrison, "A Temple for Byzantium," 129; Bardill, "Église Saint-Polyeucte," 88–91.

[214] Stroth, *Monogrammkapitelle*, pp. 110–111.   [215] Bardill, "Église Saint-Polyeucte," 88–89.

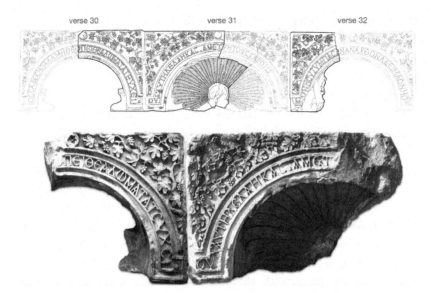

Figure 28 Three block of the Great Entablature with verses 30–32 are matching (Stroth 2015 after Harrison, Excavations, 120 Fig. B)

Therefore, it seems reasonable to focus the observations on the two central exedrae, and here the findings speak a clear language, Each of the six preserved blocks bears one verse of the founder's epigram, the large niche blocks on the sides two verses each (Figure 17).[216]

This distribution of the poem is closely related to the processing of the inscribed marble blocks, which already took place on the ground, that is, before the individual blocks were moved to their final place in the building. Research long assumed that the carving of the entablature and of the inscription has taken place as one of the finishing stages, in situ, as it can be shown for Sts. Sergius and Bacchus (Figure 18).[217] But at St. Polyeuktos, things are different; the elaborate relief and the distribution of the verses on the individual blocks speak for a carving on the ground.[218]

The exedrae constructed in this way were flanked by niches whose shape can also be reliably reconstructed by further fragments.[219] For the northern central exedra, the fragment of such a niche with the beginning of verse 27 has been preserved, so that its position to the left of the northern exedra can be traced.[220] For the southern exedra a fragment with the end of verse 9 has been preserved

---

[216] Bardill, "Église Saint-Polyeucte," 89.

[217] Harrison, *Excavator, vol. 1*, p. 414; Connor 1999, 505.

[218] Stroth, *Monogrammkapitelle*, p. 106.   [219] Kakko, *Gebälkstücke*, pp. 18–35.

[220] Harrison, *Excavations, vol. 1*, pp. 117–119, Kat. 1a iv, Abb. 94, 95.

(Figure 22).[221] Accordingly, each of these flanking niches has included two lines of the epigram, the beginning on the left (verse 27) and the end on the right (verse 9) of which can be traced in the archaeological findings. Also the transition of the verses at the arch apex of such a niche has been preserved on a fragment of the southern exedra with remains of verses 15 and 16 (Figure 27).[222] Soffits prove that the undersides of the niches were visible and supported by two pillars each.[223]

Some of St. Polyeuktos' architectural elements, which traveled widely after 1204, seem to complement the excavation findings in Istanbul, fitting like the missing pieces of a puzzle. However, the archaeological excavations were able to clarify unmistakably that the pillars placed next to St Mark's Basilica in Venice since the thirteenth century were not suitable as supports for the main order on the ground floor of the Polyeuktos Church (Figure 3). A pillar capital, distinguished by its unusual size and singular decoration with a central date palm motif, was found fallen into the substructures during the excavations, together with an inscribed marble block and the fragment of the marble revetment of an associated pillar (Figure 22).[224] These pieces of the main order are about 25 percent larger than the corresponding pieces in Venice and show significant differences in decoration.[225] Later findings in the Mangana region suggest that we should reconstruct the pillars of the main order not as massive marble blocks like the *pilastri acritani* are, but rather as bricked-up structures that were covered with decorated marble slabs.[226]

From the group of multiform capital types known for St. Polyeuktos, only the capital in Barcelona meets the size requirements for the *exedrae* of the ground floor.[227] In addition, a stylistic connection between the Barcelona-type capitals and the excavated pillar capitals is achieved by means of the protruding cornucopia bands on the diagonals, even though these fragile reliefs today are largely broken or have been reworked (Figures 3 and 22).[228] These unusual details, which shape the overall impression of the capitals, have received little attention in research and thus remain enigmatic.

---

[221] Harrison, *Excavations, vol. 1*, p. 117, No. 1ai.

[222] Harrison, *Excavations, vol. 1*, p. 117, Kat. 1a ii, Abb. 91. 92.

[223] Harrison, *Excavations, vol. 1*, p. 117, Kat. 1a ii, Abb. 92. Compare also Harrison, "A Temple for Byzantium," 126, fig. 167.

[224] Harrison, *Excavations, vol. 1*, p. 132, Kat. 5b[i]. 133, Kat, 6b[i], 409; Ders. 1989, 58, fig. 54; 59, fig. 55. 56; compare Bardill, "Église Saint-Polyeucte," 92n13.

[225] Harrison, *Excavations, vol. 1*, p. 133.

[226] Tunay, "Byzantine Archaeological Findings," 223–224, Fig. 10.

[227] Harrison, *Excavations, vol. 1*, p. 409; Kakko, *Gebälkstücke*, 91–93.

[228] Harrison *Excavations, vol. 1*, fig. 133, 142, 150.

In an attempt to establish a connection between these *exedrae* and the overall building, the latter of which is preserved only in its substructures, all previous reconstruction proposals show weaknesses and do not fit within the realm of profound archaeological argumentation.[229] The reverse connection of the *exedra* rows to the church's side aisles remains a riddle. Significant reworking on the backs of the prominent inscription blocks could provide essential insights in this regard, but so far has received no attention in context of the study of the building.[230]

Another specific architectural problem that arises from the reconstruction of St. Polyeuktos with a wooden roof has similarly received little attention so far. How was it possible to integrate the large *exedrae* into the side aisles structurally? While in a standard basilica the clerestory consists of two simple upper walls, the unique interior design of St. Polyeuktos complicated things. The rows of *exedrae* on both sides of the *naos* ended in half domes of considerable size (Figure 5 and 7). These vaults of about 7–8 meters would have caused lateral forces and required structural integration into the side aisles. Alternatively, we know of wooden half domes, such as the apse of the Church of St. Stephen in Gaza.[231] A dropped wooden ceiling over the galleries of the side aisles could have covered the back part of the vaults.

In summary, despite a highly fragmentary tradition, scholarship on the reconstruction of the *exedrae* has come surprisingly far. The unique and fortunate interlocking of architectural elements and documents in Istanbul, Barcelona, and Heidelberg allows us to reconstruct two *exedrae* of St. Polyeuktos reliably. This allows us to reconstruct the position of verses 8–16 as well as 27–35 as facing each other in the center of the church space. In this way, questions about the spatial references of the epigram become possible. The six marble blocks with remains of the epigram make it conceivable that one line of the epigram was placed on each block. The verse-per-block principle provided a method for transferring the poem to the stone that allowed several stonemasons to work on several blocks at the same time and similarly, largely eliminated errors in the connections of the epigram verses.

9 No Temple for Byzantium

Prominently exhibited in the title of his book *A Temple for Byzantium*, the excavator, Martin Harrison, promoted the idea that St. Polyeuktos was intended to replicate the biblical *Templum Salomonis*.[232] This interpretation has been a popular and enduring narrative for St. Polyeuktos and has received a lively

---

[229] Parment, *Alternative Reconstruction*; Bardill, "A New Temple"; ibid. "Église Saint-Polyeucte"; Kakko, *Gebälkstücke*.

[230] Harrison, *A Temple for Byzantium*, fig. 101, 103.   [231] Maguire, "'Half-Cone' Vault."

[232] Harrison, "Church of St. Polyeuktos"; Harrison, "Source for Anicia Juliana," 141–142; Harrison, *Excavations, vol. 1*, p. 410; Harrison, *A Temple for Byzantium*, p. 137–144.

response in the academic community and beyond.[233] Although the Jewish Temple of Jerusalem had disappeared long before the Byzantine period, its shadow loomed large.

Indeed, the basic features, proportions, and dimensions of the Temple were known from a variety of sources.[234] In the sixth century there was a trend toward increased references to biblical history and Byzantine rhetoricians often used allegorical relations between Byzantine churches and the Old Testament Temple as a topos.[235] But in contrast to textual and metaphorical imagery, St. Polyeuktos is understood by scholars to be a physical replica in its design, measurements, and decoration. Despite wide acceptance and enthusiasm for this idea, the arguments supporting it are surprisingly weak.

The Epigram of St. Polyeuktos Mentioning Solomon

The adulatory inscription at the western façade of the church provides the first argument supporting Harrison's Temple interpretation. After praising the emperors Constantine and Theodosius as the great builders in the City's history (see Section 6), the text on the second inscription panel claims that the foundress Anicia Juliana:

> alone has conquered time and surpassed the wisdom of the celebrated Solomon, raising a temple to receive God, the richly wrought and graceful splendor of which the ages cannot celebrate.[236]

The image of the Old Temple was still very much present in sixth-century Constantinople; in fact, textual references to Solomon occur frequently during this time. For the Hagia Sophia alone, we can point to several texts illustrating this tendency.[237] The hymn "On Earthquakes and Fires," which was very likely recited for the first time shortly before the official re-inauguration of Justinian's Hagia Sophia in 537, is one of these examples:[238]

---

[233] Harrison, *A Temple for Byzantium*; Scheja, "Hagia Sophia"; Harrison, "Church of St. Polyeuktos"; ibid., *A Temple for Byzantium*; ibid., "Jerusalem and Back Again"; Vickers, "A 'New' Capital"; Milner, "Rightful Ruler"; Fowden, "Constantine, Silvester and the Church"; Koder, "Sieg über Salomon"; Sodini, "Les paons de Saint-Polyeucte"; Connor, "Epigram in the Church"; Bardill, *Brickstamps*; Shahîd, "New Observations," 343–355; Nathan, "Architectural Narratology"; Whitby, "A Literary Perspective"; Bardill, "A New Temple," 365; "Église Saint-Polyeucte," 2011; Koder, "Imperial Propaganda," 279; Ousterhout, "New Temples and New Solomons"; Viermann, "Surpassing Solomon."

[234] For the descriptions see 1 Kings 6; 7:13–51; 2 Chronicles 3–4; Ezekiel 40–48; Ezra 1–6; Josephus, Jewish Wars 5, among others.

[235] Wilkinson, "Paulinus' Temple," 553–561; Krueger, "Christian Piety," 295.

[236] *AP* 1.10, 48–50; Harrison, *Excavations, vol. 1*, pp. 5–7.   [237] Scheja, "Hagia Sophia."

[238] Catafygiotu Topping, "On Earthquakes and Fires," 22–25; Koder, "Imperial Propaganda," 278–280.

Remember Jerusalem and its mighty temple: The all-wise king Solomon, over a very long period, built and adorned that temple at a countless cost. Yet it was destroyed and exposed to derision. It remains fallen. It has not risen again. From this, one understands the grace of the church, which gives eternal life. The people of Israel lost their Temple. In its place we now have the churches of the Resurrection and Sion, which Constantine and the faithful Helena gave to the world, two hundred and fifty years after the destruction of the Temple.

But here in the Imperial City people began the task of raising the church only one day after their fall. [. . .] The emperor and empress are proud of their generosity; but it is the Lord who gives eternal life.

The references to Solomon in both texts – the epigram of Juliana's church as well as the hymn to Justinian's Hagia Sophia – follow a similar pattern. On the one hand, Solomon functions as a biblical archetype for a good founder of a monumental sacred building, hereby providing a suitable typological comparison for the dedicatees in these dedicatory texts. It is no coincidence that both texts also refer to Emperor Constantine as the City's most important historical founder. On the other hand, both texts emphasize the difference in durability between the original temple and its successors. Unlike Solomon's temple, which was destroyed and lost, both church buildings in Constantinople had been constructed rather quickly and were splendid re-creations of older sanctuaries, intended to last through the centuries.[239] Thus, the Temple of Solomon served both as a metaphorical role model and a means of contrast.[240]

Christine Milner, and Jonathan Bardill at a later date, modified Harrison's Temple idea and argued that the *specific* model for Juliana's church was rather Ezekiel's Temple and that she intended "an earthly copy of a new and better Temple"[241] surpassing Solomon's work. This is rather difficult to argue, since the dedicatory inscription refers explicitly and exclusively to Solomon himself.

The Measurements

The excavator, Martin Harrison, has argued that the sanctuary of St. Polyeuktos replicated the Temple of Solomon in its exact measurements as given in the Book of Kings or Ezekiel.[242] His idea was not entirely new. In the case of Hagia Sophia, earlier attempts had been made to apply metaphorical Solomonic

---

[239] Meier, *Das andere Zeitalter Justinians*, 82–83.

[240] On the many references to Solomon from the sixth century to the Byzantine middle ages cf. Cameron, *Corripus*, pp. 204–205; Dagron, *Constantinople imaginaire*, pp. 303–306; Prinzing, "Das Bild Justinians," 89–91; Koder, "Justinians Sieg," 135–138; Ousterhout, "New Temples and New Solomons"; Viermann, "Surpassing Solomon," 215–216.

[241] Milner, "Rightful Ruler," 73–81; Bardill, "A New Temple," 341–345.

[242] Harrison, "The Church of St. Polyeuktos," 276–279; Harrison, *Excavations, vol. 1*, pp. 410–411.

references in Byzantine texts as the actual unit of measurement of the building.[243] While no current scholars believe this to be true for the Church of Justinian, the idea is still very common for St. Polyeuktos. Upon taking a closer look, however, the measurements and relations are not any more convincing for Juliana's church.

For St. Polyeuktos, the length and width of the church given by the excavators is approximately 52 x 52 meters, which can be divided quite well into 100 x 100 royal cubits of 0.52 meters (Figure 10). At first glance, this seems to fit neatly with biblical references to the Temple. Unfortunately, these calculations are not quite that simple, and for such a numbers game to work, the textual and archaeological data has to be interpreted very selectively. The square of space taken as a basis by the excavators can only be achieved if the *naos* and the naves are measured together, while the narthex in front must be excluded. Structurally, however, there are no good reasons to consider the latter structure separately. Not only is the sub-narthex part of the church's platform and integral to its structure, but the central corridor and narthex share the complex system of cross vaultings and thus have certainly been designed and constructed together. If one measures the full main body of the church together with the narthex, one obtains a less conspicuous basic dimension of 58 x 52 meters.

Finally, the dimensions deviate from the actual Temple dimensions as given in the Bible. Ezekiel reports the length of the Temple as 100 cubits, while the width, however, was only 20 cubits. Only for the platform of the Temple is a width of 100 cubits reported.

We have good reason to believe that the idea of St. Polyeuktos being a physical model of the temple in terms of its dimensions originates in an idea broached in a Dumbarton Oaks peer review. Harrison's originally submitted manuscript for the final monograph does not seem to have mentioned this idea at all. The anonymous peer reviewer of the manuscript, however, offered among other things the following suggestion:

> One additional area of investigation that might well prove rewarding in elucidating the groundplan and elevation is that of modules. What was the basic unit of design? A building of this complexity must surely have been planned around such a unit. An hour or two with a calculator might yield some interesting statistics.[244]

The fact that Harrison started to deal with the subject only at this late date, when the field work at Saraçhane was already finished, is of interest for us. The metrology of the structure – which was never explained in detail at any

---

[243] Scheja, "Hagia Sophia," 54; Stache, *Corripus*, p. 541.

[244] Saraçhane Excavation Archive, University of Oxford.

point – could not have been deduced from the original walls, but rather was developed as a product of armchair-archaeology. Finally, it seems to have been Michael Vickers who first offered the idea that the unit of measurement was not the usual "Byzantine feet" but could have been the so-called "royal cubit."[245] Vickers was involved in archaeological fieldwork in Northern Africa, where the team had encountered a local unit of measurement, the "Punic foot," for the layout of second-century Roman military buildings in Tripolitania.[246] While the use of traditional units of measurement by local craftsmen in Tripolitania is plausible for practical reasons, it is hard to imagine a workshop in Constantinople giving up its established workflow to engage in virtual measurements for such complex architecture.

Robert Ousterhout sums it up brilliantly when he states that any Byzantine church can become an image of the Temple simply by appropriating its terminology.[247] A reference to the Temple is made through words, ceremonies, and relics, but not through specific architectural forms or measurements.

The Architectural Sculpture (Peacocks for Seraphs)

Similarly, the ostentatious decoration of St. Polyeuktos has been compared with that described for the Temple. Harrison points to the church's interior decoration, especially the omnipresent peacock motif. The peacocks in the niches of the lower *exedra* were interpreted as reference of the cherubim which, according to the Book of Kings and Ezekiel, adorned the Temple.[248] Methodologically, this is poorly done art history and requires no lengthy contradiction; a peacock is not a cherub. Later advocates of the Temple thesis agreed that such an interpretation is problematic, preferring instead to interpret the iconography of the interior decoration of St. Polyeuktos characterized by its peacocks and palm trees as a more general reference to paradise.[249]

In conclusion, the tempting idea that Anicia Juliana's church was meant to be a physical copy of the biblical Temple – whether that of Solomon or of Ezekiel – is not convincing. The brief reference to the biblical builder Solomon in the very long epigram of St. Polyeuktos is not a special feature or even a unique attribute, but rather one contemporary metaphorical strategy to praise the foundress and her building. The fact that Byzantine poets used a similar image of Solomon to praise both Juliana and Justinian should not be understood as a contest or conflict between the two, but rather as an indication of how popular and widespread this topos already was. Even on a metaphorical level, the allusions

---

[245] Harrison, "Church of St. Polyeuktos," p. 277n7.

[246] Humphrey, Sear, and Vickers, "Aspects of the Circus," 47, 91.

[247] Ousterhout, "New Temples and New Solomons," 252.

[248] Harrison, *Excavations, vol. 1*, pp. 410–411, p. 416.   [249] Bardill, "A New Temple," 344.

ultimately fall short of the mark. The dedicatory poem as a whole does not support this kind of interpretation of the building. The text contains no sophisticated theological content, let alone any eschatological allusions.[250] What emerges from the text, instead, is Juliana's ambition to create a monument that would endure throughout the ages and prove worthy of herself and of her ancestors for all time.[251] This is the key point of comparison the poet of Juliana's epigram wanted to highlight with these references to Solomon's lost Temple, and it is equally appropriate when applied to Justinian's Hagia Sophia.

10 The Site in the Middle Ages

Apart from the magnificent archaeological finds and exciting questions about the sixth-century building, very little attention has been paid to the medieval use of the site. The mention of St. Polyeuktos as a station on the imperial procession for Easter Mondays in the *Book of Ceremonies* attests that the church was still intact in the second half of the tenth century.[252] Likewise, the commentator of the tenth-century *Anthologia Palatina* describes the building as being "in excellent condition."[253] The last reference to St. Polyeuktos as a still-intact church is an anonymous pilgrimage report dating to the early eleventh century.[254] Soon after, an earthquake is suspected to have destroyed the main structure.

We are relatively poorly informed about the period in between. The excavations yielded hardly any findings on subsequent alterations or additions to the structure. An unexpectedly plentiful series of coins of the eighth century stands in contrast to their near-total absence in excavated provincial cities. The pottery of Saraçhane has also proved to be key to our understanding of the Dark Ages thanks to the relentless and brilliant research work of John Hayes.[255]

The Marble Icons

The most important group of Early Medieval finds from St. Polyeuktos is a group of eight marble panels with figural relief decoration (Figure 29).[256] While the excavator considered them to be parts of the original sixth-century equipment of the church, there is broad consensus today that they came into

---

[250] Viermann, "Surpassing Solomon," 222–223.   [251] Ibid.

[252] *De Ceremoniis* I.10. Effenberger, "Venezianischen Tetrarchengruppen," 243–245.

[253] *AP* 1.10.

[254] Ciggaar, "Une description de Constantinople," 211–267; Harrison, *Excavations, vol. 1*, p. 10.

[255] Hayes, *The Pottery*.

[256] Harrison and Fıratlı, "Second and Third Preliminary Reports," 235, Fig. 33–38; Harrison and Fıratlı, "Fifth Preliminary Report," 199; Harrison, *Excavations, vol. 1*, pp. 156–157, Fig. 197–206; Harrison, *A Temple for Byzantium*, p. 109, fig. 135–142; Fıratlı, *Sculpture byzantine figurée*, pp. 208–211, no. 485–493.

Figure 29 Marble icon with Apostle (Credit: Mathews – Muller, *Dawn of Christian Art*, Fig. 6.9)

the church at a later stage.[257] The panels measure about 40 x 35 x 10 centimeters and show a bust image of Christ, the Mother of God and a set of saints, who are depicted either with veiled hands, with gemmed codices, or carrying a cross.

Differences in the manner in which the heads, hands, and robes were made suggest that three stonemasons were involved in the production.[258]

All figures are shown frontally, and the faces and hands seem to have fallen victim to systematic damage. This damage is associated with the Byzantine iconoclastic controversy, so we can safely posit the eighth century as a *terminus ante quem*. Shortly after their excavation, the interpretation of these panels as icons of the early Byzantine *templon* of the church was already being raised.[259] However, this interpretation is problematic for several reasons.[260]

The quality and style of the marble carving is clearly different from the other sculptures in the church.[261] A dating of the reliefs into the seventh century is

---

[257] Nees, "Iconographic Program," 18–19; Harrison, *Excavations, vol. 1*, p. 418; Belting, *Bild und Kult*, p. 266; Russo, "Architettura e scultura," 74; Mathews and Muller, *Dawn of Christian Art*, p. 173.

[258] Fıratlı, *Sculpture byzantine figurée*, pp. 208–209; Kiilerich, "Reconsidering the Figural Marble Panels," 43.

[259] Grabar, "Recherches sur les sculptures," 38–41; Chatzidakis, "L'évolution de l'icone," 330; Harrison, *Excavations, vol. 1*, p. 418; Mathews and Muller, *Dawn of Christian Art*; Mathews, "Origins of Icons," 27.

[260] Mango, "Storia del arte," 316–321; Peschlow, "Review of Harrison 1989," 629–630; Parpulov, "Review of Mathews and Muller 2016," 62–63.

[261] Parpulov, "Review of Mathews and Muller 2016," 62–63.

stylistically convincing.[262] Thus, if one would assume a function of the images in the *templon*, they would necessarily have been later additions.[263]

Technical traces have been pointed out as small square holes at the bottom of the front of all panels, which are either interpreted as fastening traces, or would have been used to fasten lamps.[264] Plaster remains on the outer edges indicate that at least some of the panels were originally framed by stucco.[265]

So far, too little attention has been paid to the finding place of the plates within the structure in two opposite places in the northern and southern part of the sub-narthex of the church.[266] The distance between the finding location and the *bema* of the church has been explained so far by the fact that the slabs could have been moved to the substructure of the narthex after iconoclastically motivated damage and deposited there.[267] However, one could also consider that the images were already present in this place. Here was the entrance to the connecting corridor between the atrium and the crypt, and so, the images could well have fulfilled a function in this place as well.[268]

While the image panels of the Polyeuktos church were long considered to be early isolated finds, very similar objects have since become known at other sites. A group of altogether seven marble image panels of similar format, but different techniques, came to light in a church in Olympos and is not addressed by the excavators as icons of the *templon*, but reconstructed as having been placed on a side wall in the *naos*.[269]

---

[262] Mango, "Storia del arte," 316–321; Grabar, "Recherches sur les sculptures," 38–41; Belting, *Bild und Kult*, p. 266; Parpulov, "Review of Mathews and Muller 2016," 62–63.

[263] Moreover, for a building like the Polyeuktos Church, one may rather think of a templon made of precious metal, as it is also transmitted for the Hagia Sophia. On the other hand, Paulos Silentiarios explicitly points out that for the barrier of the Hagia Sophia – apparently different from usual – "neither ivory, nor cut stone work or ore" had been used (καὶ γὰρ ὅσον μεγάλοιο πρὸς ὄρθιον ἄντυγα νηοῦ χῶρον ἀναιμάκτοισιν ἀπεκρίναντο θυηλαῖς, οὐκ ἐλέφας᾽μ οὐ τμῆμα λίθων ἢ χαλκὸς ὁρίζει), Paulos Silentiarios, *Ekphrasis* 682–685, trans. Veh, p. 341.

[264] Harrison, *Excavations, vol. 1*, p. 156; Nees, "Iconographic Program," 18; Mathews and Muller, *Dawn of Christian Art*, pp. 179–181.

[265] For pictures of the stucco remains see Nees, "Iconographic Program," 17, fig. 3; Mathews and Muller, *Dawn of Christian Art*, pp. 178–179, fig. 6.12. 6.14; The reconstruction of the panels in Mathews – Muller 2016, 181, 8.18. is wrong, because accidentally broken edges are here misunderstood as part of the framing.

[266] On the noticeable finding position of the panels in the northern (U/16) and in the southern area (T/19) of the narthex see Harrison and Fıratlı, "Second and Third Preliminary Reports," 235; Harrison, *Excavations, vol. 1*; A storage of the plates in the building without any relation to the church of Anicia Juliana assumes Kiilerich, "Reconsidering the Figural Marble Panels," 39, 44.

[267] Harrison, *A Temple for Byzantium*, p. 109; Mathew and Muller, *Dawn of Christian Art*, p. 173.

[268] However, a rectangular recess in the north wall of the sub-narthex is out of the question for this purpose because of its too large size of 100 x 70 centimeters. Harrison, *Excavations, vol. 1*, p. 23, fig. F; fig. 37.

[269] The total of seven marble panels of about 25 x 25 centimeters came to light in the so-called Basilica III in Olympos, a building whose main phase can be placed in the sixth century. One bust can be identified as Paul thanks to a titulus. Olcay Uçkan and Öztaşkin, "Olympos

The question whether the relief panels of the Polyeuktos church are really images of the *templon* barriers and thus early archaeological evidence of this image practice must therefore be doubted.[270] Although the characters depicted in the reliefs can be easily compared with the description of the *templon* of Hagia Sophia, the material execution remains different in crucial points.

The Cemetery and the Funerary Column

In the middle Byzantine era, the atrium became a cemetery. As the excavation was a rescue dig, the cemetery was not dug under ideal conditions and not all graves were recorded. A total of 143 burials are listed by Harrison. A complication was the disturbance of the cemetery in later Byzantine and Turkish times. As a result, Harrison acknowledges that it is not possible to determine a chronological sequence for the graves. Eric Ivison was able to clarify some points of chronology and to establish reliable dates for the use of the cemetery.

The chronology of the cemetery in the atrium can best be understood by examining the levels over the staircase leading up to church, and the pavement immediately in front of it. In the late tenth and early eleventh centuries, black earth began to accumulate on the pavement of the atrium, washed up by rainfall. This indicates that the drains were blocked and that the church and its perimeter were dilapidated or abandoned. Such abandonment led to the despoliation of the church for its marble, including the destruction of the steps and railings of the staircase. The looted foundation of the stairs was then covered with earth containing a ceramic mixture, the most recent finds of which date to the first half of the twelfth century.

The cemetery must have been founded by 1150, for nearly all the burials were dug into fills containing pottery of no later than the first half of the twelfth century: The graves were dug into these layers and so therefore must be even later than them. This twelfth-century date is also confirmed by the dates of objects found associated with the burials.

The coin series from the site suggests to Michael Hendy that the site was certainly in ruins by about 1225, perhaps as a result of the final collapse of the church.

In the last days of excavation, some 5 meters west of the entrance staircase of the church, the circular pedestal for a columned monument was unearthed.

Excavations 2018," 231; Olcay Uçkan et al., "Olympos Kazisi 2017 Yili Çalişmalari," 626–627, fig. 8. In Hanita, Israel, the fragment of a comparable tablet has become known, which is also dated to the sixth century; see Barasch, "A Relief at Hanita," 474–482.

[270] Olcay Uçkan and Öztaşkin, "Olympos Excavations 2018," 231; Olcay Uçkan et al., "Olympos Kazisi 2017 Yili Çalişmalari," 626–627, fig. 8.

Figure 30 Postament of the Funerary Column of St. Polyeuktos. At a later stage, the monument itself got buried under later graves. (Credit: Saraçhane Excavation Archive, University of Oxford)

This monument has received little attention so far, although it is a unique find for the Byzantine Funerary archaeology of Constantinople (Figures 30 and 31)

The structure was built on top of the accumulated earth in the atrium, and so probably has a terminus post quem of circa 1100–1150. What has survived is a circular base with a diameter of 3 meters. The intensive reuse of marble fragments for the lowest layer of this base indicates the desire for a solid foundation. At the top, a column base measuring approx. 1 x 1 meters was embedded between marble slabs in the center of the circular construction. A precisely worked 40 cm profile enclosed the top and slightly set off like a round stylobate. Traces and dowel holes on this round stylobate allow the reconstruction of curved barrier slabs set on top of it, which were embedded between six posts. The format of the monolithic column base suggests an erected column shaft above of more than 5 meters. This results in a funerary column of impressive size.

The excavator Harrison is right to interpret the construction as a graveyard-marker erected in the middle Byzantine cemetery only at the twelfth century.[271] No comparison has yet been mentioned for this monument yet, but one can point to a similar, albeit clearly smaller construction

---

[271] Harrison *Excavations, vol. 1*, 27. fig. 76–78; Thiel, *Die Johanneskirche*, pp. 19–20, plate 21 a–c;.

St. Polyeuktos in Constantinople
(after sketchbook of G. Lawson 1965)

St. John in Ephesos
(after A. Thiel 2005)

Figure 31 The Funerary Columns of St. Polyeuktos and of St. John in Ephesos
in comparison (Credit: Drawing by D. Miznazi 2022)

in the atrium of the Basilica of St John in Ephesus (Figure 31). Here, too,
the courtyard of the church is used as a cemetery in middle Byzantine times
and a column monument of moderate size is erected. Even in its late phase
of use, with the funerary column of St. Polyeuktos, the site once again
holds an otherwise unknown type of monument for the archaeology of
Constantinople.

Bibliography

Agosti G., "Versus *De Limine* and *In Limine*: Displaying Greek paideia at the Entrance of Early Christian Churches," in E. M. Van Opstall (ed.), *Sacred Thresholds: The Door to the Sanctuary in Late Antiquity* (Boston: Brill, 2018), 254–281.

Agosti G., "Metrical Inscriptions in Late Antiquity: What Difference Did Christianity Make?" in F. Hadjittofi and A. Lefteratou (eds.), *The Genres of Late Antique Christian Poetry: Between Modulations and Transpositions* (Berlin: De Gruyter, 2020), 39–58

Agosti G. and F. Gonelli, "Materiali per la storia dell'esametro nei poeti cristiani greci," in M. Fantuzzi and R. Pretagostini (eds.), *Struttura e storia dell'esametro greco* (Rome: Gruppo Editoriale Internazionale, 1995), 289–434

Arthur P. R., "Review to Hayes 1992," *Gnomon* 66 (1994), 474–476

Asgari N., "Edirnekapı Başlığı," *Arkeoloji ve Sanat* 1 (1975), 14–17

Barasch M., "A Relief from the Early Byzantine Period at Hanita," in M. Yedaya (ed.), *The Western Galilee Antiquities* (Tel Aviv: Ministry of Defense Press, 1986), 474–482

Bardill J., "A New Temple for Byzantium: Anicia Juliana, King Solomon, and the gilded ceiling of the church of St. Polyeuktos in Constantinople," *Late Antique Archaeology* 3/1 (2006), 339–370

Bardill J., "Église Saint-Polyeucte à Constantinople: nouvelle solution pour l'énigme de sa reconstitution," in J.-M. Spieser (ed.), *Architecture Paléochrétienne* (Gollion: Infolio, 2011), 77–103

Bardill J., "The Church of Sts. Sergius and Bacchus in Constantinople and the Monophysite Refugees," *Dumbarton Oaks Papers* 54 (2000), 1–11

Bardill J., *Brickstamps of Constantinople* (Oxford: Oxford University Press, 2004)

Barsanti C., "Venezia e Costantinopoli: capitelli di reimpiego nelle dimore lagunari del Duecento," in E. Concina, G. Trovabene, and M. Agazzi (eds.), *Hadriatica. Attorno a Venezia e al Medioevo tra arti, storia e storiografia. Scritti in onore di Wladimiro Dorigo* (Padua: Il Poligrafo, 2002), 59–69

Barsanti C. and M. Pilutti Namer, "Da Costantinopoli a Venezia: nuove spoglie della chiesa di S. Polieucto. Nota preliminare," *Nea Rhome* 6 (2009), 133–156

Bauer J., "Zu den christlichen Gedichten der Anthologia Graeca," *JÖB* 9 (1960), 31–40

Beckby H., *Anthologia Graeca* (München: Tusculum-Bücherei, 1965)

Beckwith J., *Early Christian and Byzantine Art* (New Haven: Yale University Press, 1986)

Bell P. N., *Social Conflict in the Age of Justinian: Its Nature, Management, and Mediation* (Oxford: Oxford University Press, 2013)

Belting H., *Bild und Kult. Die Geschichte des Bildes vor dem Zeitalter der Kunst* (München: C. H. Beck, 1990)

Berger A., *Accounts of Medieval Constantinople: The Patria*, Dumbarton Oaks Medieval Library (Cambridge, MA: Harvard University Press, 2013a)

Berger A., "Mokios und Konstantin der Große. Zu den Anfängen des Märtyrerkultes in Konstantinopel," in V. A. Leontaritou, K. A. Bourdara, and E. S. Papagianni (eds.), *Antecessor: Festschrift für Spyros N. Troianos* (Athens: Ekdoseis Ant. N. Sakkoula, 2013b), 165–185

Bertelli C., "Lastra scolpita," in M. T. Fiorio (ed.), *Museo d'Arte Antica del Castello Sforzesco. Scultura lapidea 1* (Milan: Electa, 2012), 42–43

Bertelli C., "Spigolature bizantine in un museo Milano," in F. D'Arcais and M. Olivari (eds.), *Arte lombarda del secolo millenio. Saggi in onore di Gian Alberto Dell'Acqua* (Milan: F. Motta, 2000), 16–21

Bertelli C., "Transenna frammentaria da Agios Polieuktos," in C. Bertelli and A. Augenti (eds.), *Santi, Banchieri e Re. Ravenna e Classe nel VI secolo San Severo e il tempio ritrovato* (Milan: Skira, 2006), 131

Bittel K., "Funde byzantinischer Zeit. A. Forschungen und Funde in Istanbul. Arbeiten im Gebiet der Sophienkirche: Grabung der Abteilung Istanbul; Grabung im Hof des Top Kapi Sarayi," *Jahrbuch des deutschen archäologischen Instituts* 54/1–2 (1939), 176–182

Bogdanović J., *The Framing of Sacred Space: The Canopy and the Byzantine Church* (Oxford: Oxford University Press, 2017)

Brands G., "Persien und Byzanz – Eine Annäherung," in F. Pirson and U. Wulff-Rheidt (eds.), *Austausch und Inspiration: Kulturkontakte als Impuls architektonischer Innovation*, DiskAB 9 (Mainz am Rhein: von Zabern, 2006), 244–256

Brandt O., "Understanding the Structures of Early Christian Basilicas," in D. Hellmholm, T. Vegge, Ø. Norderval, and Ch. Hellholm (eds.), *Ablution, Initiation, and Baptism: Late Antiquity, Early Judaism, and Early Christianity* (Boston: De Gruyter, 2011), 1587–1609

Brenk B., *Spätantike und frühes Christentum*, Propylen Kunstgeschichte 15 (Frankfurt am Main: Propyläen-Verlag, 1977)

Brüx R., "Zur sassanidischen Ornamentik in der frühbyzantinischen Kunst. Sichtungen nach Motivrepertoire, historischem Umfeld und Vermittlungswegen unter besonderer Berücksichtigung der Hagios Polyeuktos in Konstantinopel," in *Faltkapitelle: Untersuchungen zur Bauskulptur*

Konstantinopels mit einem Anhang zur Hagios Polyeuktos in Istanbul (Langenweißbach: Beier & Beran, 2008), 299–371

Cameron A., *The Greek Anthology from Meleager to Planudes* (Oxford: Clarendon Press, 1993)

Cameron Av., "The Byzantine Sources of Gregory of Tours," *The Journal of Theological Studies* 26/2 (1975), 421–426

Cameron Av., *Flavius Cresconius Corippus: In laudem Iustini Augisti minoris libri IV* (London: The Athlone Press, 1976)

Canepa M. P., *The Two Eyes of the Earth: Art and Ritual of Kingship between Rome and Sasanian Iran* (Berkely: University of California Press, 2009)

Castelfranchi M. F., "L'edificio battesimale a Constantinopoli," in I. Foletti and S. Romano (eds.), *Fons Vitae: Baptême, Baptistères at Rites d'initiation (IIe–VIe siècle)* (Rome: Viella, 2009), 101–120

Catafygiotu Topping E., "On Earthquakes and Fires: Romanos' Encomium to Justinian," *BZ* 71 (1978), 22–25

Chatzidakis M., "L'évolution de l'icone aux XIe–XIIIe siècles et la transformation du templon," in *Actes du XVe Congrès international d'études byzantines, Athènes, Septembre 1976, I* (Athens: Comité d'organisation du congrès, 1979), 331–366

Ciggaar K. N., "Une description de Constantinople traduite par un pelerine anglais," *REB* 34 (1976), 26–27

Connor C. L., "The Church of Hagios Polyeuktos in Constantinople and Anicia Juliana's Quest for Immortality," in *XX Congrès international des études byzantines. Collège de France-Sorbonne 19–25 Aout 2001. Pré-actes III. Communications libres* (Paris: Comité d'organization du Xxe Congrès international des études byzantines, 2001), 303

Connor C. L., "The Epigram in the Church of Hagios Polyeuktos in Constantinople and It's Byzantine Response," *Byzantion* 69 (1999), 479–527

Cormack R., *Byzantine Art* (Oxford: Oxford University Press, 2000)

Croke B., "Justinian, Theodora, and the Church of Saints Sergius and Bacchus," *DOP* 60 (2006), 25–63

Ćurčić S., "Design and Structural Innovation in Byzantine Architecture before Hagia Sophia," in R. Mark and A. Ş. Çakmak (eds.), *Hagia Sophia from the Age of Justinian to the Present* (Cambridge: Cambridge University Press, 1992), 16–38

Cutler A., "The Perils of Polyeuktos: On the Manifestations of a Martyr in Byzantine Art, Cult and Literature," in A. Olsen Lam and R. Schroeter (eds.), *The Eloquence of Art: Essays in Honor of Henry Maguire* (London: Routledge, 2020), 91–114

Dagron G., *Constantinople imaginaire: Études sur le recueil des Patria* (Paris: Presses universitaires de France, 1984)

Dagron G. and B. Flusin, *Constantin VII Porphyrogénète: Le livre des cérémonies*, 5 Vols., Corpus fontium historiae Byzantinae 52 (Paris: Association des Amis du Centre d'Histoire et Civilisation de Byzance, 2020)

Deichmann F. W., *Corpus der Kapitelle der Kirche von San Marco zu Venedig, unter Mitarbeit von J. Kramer und U. Peschlow*, Forschungen zur Kunstgeschichte und christlichen Archäologie 12 (Wiesbaden: Steiner, 1981)

Deichmann F. W., "Decke," *RAC* 3 (1957a), 629–643

Deichmann F. W., "I pilastri acritani," *RendPontAcc* 50 (1980), 75–89

Deichmann, F. W., "Kasettendecken," *JÖB* 21 (1972b), 83–107

Deichmann F. W., "Review Krautheimer 1965," *BZ* 65 (1972a), 102–123

Deichmann F. W., *Studien zur Architektur Konstntinopels im 5. und 6. Jahrhundert nach Christus* (Baden-Baden: Bruno Grimm, 1956)

Deichmann F. W., "Untersuchung zu Dach und Decke der Basilika," in K. Schauenburg (ed.), *Charites: Studien zur Altertumswissenschaft* (Bonn: Athenäum-Verlag, 1957b), 249–264.

Deliyannis D., *Agnelli Ravennatis: Liber Pontificalis Ecclesiale Ravennatis.* Corpus Christianorum 199 (Turnhout: Brepols, 2006)

Deliyannis D., *The Book of Pontiffs of the Church of Ravenna.* Medieval Texts in Translation (Washington, DC: Catholic University of America Press, 2004)

Della Valle M., *Costantinopoli e il suo impero. Arte, architettura, urbanistica nel millennio bizantino* (Milan: Jaca Book, 2007)

Demangel M. R., *Contribution à la topographie de l'Hebdomon* (Paris: Recherches françaises en Turquie, 1945)

van Dienten J.-L., "Zur Herstellung des Codex Palat. Gr. 23/Paris. Suppl. Gr. 384," *BZ* 86/87 (1993/94), 342–362

Diez E., *Die Miniaturen des Wiener Dioskurides* (Vienna: Druck und Verlag der Mechitharisten-Kongregation in Wien, 1903)

Dirimtekin F., "Finds from the Site of the Old Square West of the Town Hall at Saraçhane," *Ayasofia Müzesi yıllığı, Annual of Ayasofya Museum* 2 (1960), 42–43

Dodd E. C., "Islamic States and the Middle East," in E. C. Schwartz (ed.), *The Oxford Handbook of Byzantine Art and Architecture* (Oxford: Oxford University Press, 2021), 201–214

Eastmond A., "Monograms and the Art of unhelpful Writing in Late Antiquity," in B. M. Bedos-Rezak and J. F. Hamburger (eds.), *Sign and Design: Script as Image in Cross-Cultural Perspective (300–1600 CE)* (Cambridge, MA: Harvard University Press 2016), 219–236

Eastmond A., *The Glory of Byzantium and Early Christendom* (London: Phaidon, 2013)

Ebersolt J., *Mission archéologique de Constantinople* (Paris: E. Leroux, 1921)

Ebersolt J. and Thiers A., *Les églises de Constantinople* (Paris: E. Leroux, 1913)

Eco U., *The Book of Legendary Lands* (New York: Rizzoli Ex Libris, 2013)

Effenberger A., "'Sasanidischer' Baudekor in Byzanz? Der Fall der Polyeuktoskirche in Konstantinopel," in N. Asutay-Effenberger and F. Daim (eds.), *Sasanian Elements in Byzantine, Caucasian and Islamic Art and Culture* (Mainz: Verlag des Römisch-Germanischen Zentralmuseums, 2019), 155–194

Effenberger A., "Zur Wiederverwendung der venezianischen Tetrarchengruppen in Konstantinopel," *Millenium Studien* 10/1 (2013), 215–274

Engemann J., *Römische Kunst in Spätantike und frühem Christentum bis Justinian* (Darmstadt: Philipp von Zabern, 2014)

Eyice S., "Le baptistère d'Saint Sophie d'Istanbul," in *Atti IX Congresso Internazionale di Archeologia Cristiana*. Vol. 2. (Vatican: Pontificio Istituto di archeologia Cristiana, 1978), 257–273

Farioli Campanati R., "Review of Strube 1984," *BZ* 80 (1987), 405–407

Fıratlı N., *La Sculpture byzantine figurée au Musée archéologique d'Istanbul*, Bibliothèque de l'institut Français d'études anatoxines d'Istanbul 30 (Paris: Librairie d'Amerique et d'Orient Adrien Maisonneuve, 1990)

Flamine M., *Opere d'arte bizantina in Lombardia. Lineamenti per un catalogo (secoli IV-XV)*, Dissertation (Milan: Università degli Studi di Milano, 2013)

Flood F. B., *The Great Mosque of Damascus: Studies on the Makings of an Umayyad Visual Culture* (Leiden: Brill, 2001)

Folleti I. and Lovino F., (ed.) *Orient oder Rom? History and Reception of a Historiographical Myth (1901–1970)* (Rome: Viella, 2018)

Forsyth G., "Architectural Notes on a Trip through Cilicia," *DOP* 11 (1957), 223–236

Fowden, G., "Constantine, Silvester and the Church of S. Polyeuktos in Constantinople," *JRA* 7 (1994), 274–284

François V., "Review of Hayes 1992," *JRA* 7 (1994), 512–519

Friedländer P., *Johannes von Gaza, Paulus Silentiarius und Prokopius von Gaza: Kunstbeschreibungen justinianischer Zeit* (Hildesheim: Olms Verlag, 1912)

Gamillscheg E., "Das Geschenk für Juliana Anicia. Überlegungen zur Struktur und Entstehung des Wiener Dioskurides," in K. Belke, E. Kislinger, A. Külzer (eds.), *Byzantina Mediterranea: Festschirft Johannes Koder* (Vienna: Böhlau, 2007) 187–195

Garipzanov I., *Graphic Signs of Authority in Late Antiquity and the Early Middle Ages, 300–900* (Oxford: Oxford University Press, 2018)

Gonosová A., "The Formation and Sources of Early Byzantine Floral Semis and Floral Diaper Pattern Reexamined," *DOP* 41 (1987), 227–237

Gough M., "The Emperor Zeno and Some Cilicia Churches," *Anatolian Studies* 22 (1972), 199–212

Gough M., *Alahan: An Early Christian Monastery in Southern Turkey* (Toronto: Pontifical Institute of Mediaeval Studies, 1985)

Grabar A., "Le rayonnement de l'art sassanide dans le monde chrétien," *Accademia Nazionale dei Lincei, Quaderno* 160 (1971), 679–707

Grabar A., "Recherches sur les sculptures de l' Hypogée des Dunes, à Poitiers, et de la crypte Saint-Paul de Jouarre," *Journal des Savants* 1 (1974), 3–43

Grabar A., *Sculptures byzantines de Constantinople* (Paris: Librairie d'Amerique et d'Orient Adrien Maisonneuve, 1963)

Gregory T. E., "Review of Harrison 1989," *JFA* 18 (1991), 245–246

Guidobaldi A. G., "Da Constantinopoli a Genova e a Varese: insolito itinerario di una scultura bizantina del VI secolo," in A. Armati, M. Cerasoli, and C. Luciani (eds.), *Alle gentili art ammaestra. Festschrift Alkistis Proiou* (Rome: Dipartimento di filologia greca e latina, Sezione bizantino-neoellenica, Università di Roma "La Sapienza," 2010), 97–124

Guidobaldi A. G., "Scultura costantinopolitana del VI secolo: I capitelli reimpiegati della Medresa della Moschea di Davent Pasha," in C. Barsanti, A. Guidobaldi, and A. Iacoini (eds.), *Milion. Studi e richerche d'arte bizantina* (Rome: Campisano, 1988), 231–244

Guyer S. and Herzfeld E., *Meriamlik und Koykos*, Monumenta Asiae minoris antiqua 2 (Manchester: Pub. for the Society by the Manchester University Press, 1930)

Hansen D. U., *Anthologia Graeca I: Bücher 1 bis 5*, Bibliothek der griechischen Literatur, Bd. 72 (Stuttgart: A. Hiersemann, 2011)

Harrison R. M., "A Constantinopolitan Capital in Barcelona," *DOP* 27 (1973), 297–300

Harrison R. M., "A Source for Anicia Juliana's Palace-Church," *Byzantia Sorbonensia* 4 (1984b), 141–142

Harrison R. M., *A Temple for Byzantium: The Discovery and Excavation of Anicia Juliana's Palace-Church in Istanbul* (Austin: University of Texas Press, 1989)

Harrison R. M., "Anicia Juliana's Church of St. Polyeuktos," *JÖB* 32/4 (1982), 436–437

Harrison R. M., "Churches and Chapels in Central Lycia," *Anatolian Studies* 13 (1963), 117–151

Harrison R. M., "Excavations at Saraçhane in Istanbul 1965," *Türk arkeoloji dergisi* 16/1, (1967a), 83–88

Harrison R. M., "Excavations at Saraçhane in Istanbul 1968," *Türk arkeoloji dergisi* 18/2 (1969c), 191–198

Harrison R. M. (ed.), *Excavations at Saraçhane in Istanbul, vol. 1: The Excavations, Structures, Architectural Decoration, Small Finds, Coins, Bones, and Molluscs* (Princeton: Princeton University Press, 1986)

Harrison R. M., "From Jerusalem and Back Again: The Fate of the Treasures of Solomon," in K. Painter (ed.), *Churches Built in Ancient Times, Recent Studies in Early Christian Archaeology* (London: Society of Antiquaries of London, 1994), 239–248

Harrison R. M., "Saraçhane kazıları. Discoveries at Saraçhane," *İstanbul Arkeoloji Müzeleri yıllığı* 15 (1969b), 147–168

Harrison R. M., "Scavi della chiesa di S. Polieucto a Istanbul," *CorsiRav* (1979), 157–162

Harrison R. M., "The Church of St. Polyeuktos in Constantinople: An Excavation Report," in *Akten des VII Internationalen Kongresses für Christliche Archäologie*, Vol. 1 (Vatikanstadt: Pontificio Istituto di archeologia cristiana, 1969a), 543–549

Harrison R. M., "The Church of St. Polyeuktos in Istanbul and the Temple of Solomon," in C. Mango (ed.), *Okeanos: Essays Presented to Ihor Ševčenko on His 60th Birthday by His Colleagues and Students* (Cambridge, MA: Ukrainian Research Institute, 1984a), 276–279

Harrison R. M., "The Inscriptions and Chronology of Alahan," in M. Gough (ed.), *Alahan: An Early Christian Monastery in Southern Turkey* (Toronto: Pontifical Institute of Mediaeval Studies, 1985), 21–34

Harrison R. M., "The Monastery of Mahres Dağ in Isauria," in *Yayla, Third Report of the Northern Society for Anatolian Archaeology* (Newcastle upon Tyne: Department of Archaeology of the University of Newcastle upon Tyne, 1980), 22–24

Harrison R. M., "The Sculptural Decoration of the Church of Polyeuktos," in *Actas del VIII Congreso Internacional de Arquelogía Cristiana* (Barcelona: Consejo Superior de Investigaciones Científicas, 1972), 325–326.

Harrison R. M., "1964 yılı Saraçhane kazıları. Excavations at Saraçhane in Istanbul 1964," *Türk arkeoloji dergisi* 13/2 (1964), 106–115

Harrison R. M., "1966 yılında Istanbul'da Saraçhanede yapılan hafriyat. Excavations at Saraçhane in Istanbul 1966," *Türk arkeoloji dergisi* 16/2 (1967b), 99–102

Harrison R. M., "1964–1965 Saraçhane araştırmaları. Discoveries at Saraçhane 1964–1965," *İstanbul Arkeoloji Müzeleri yıllığı* 13, (1967c), 57–63; 128–134

Harrison R. M. and N. Fıratlı, "Excavations at Saraçhane in Istanbul: First Preliminary Report', *DOP* 19 (1965), 230–236

Harrison R. M. and N. Fıratlı, "Excavations at Saraçhane in Istanbul Second and Third Preliminary Reports," *DOP* 20 (1966a), 222–238

Harrison R. M. and N. Fıratlı, "Excavations at Saraçhane in Istanbul: Fourth Preliminary Report," *DOP* 21 (1967), 273–278

Harrison R. M. and N. Fıratlı, "Excavations at Saraçhane in Istanbul: Fifth Preliminary Report," *DOP* 22 (1968), 195–216

Harrison R. M. and N. Fıratlı, "1964–1965 Saraçhane Araştırmaları – Discoveries at Saraçhane 1964–1965," *IAMY* 13/14 (1966b), 57–63 and 128–134

Hayes J. W., *Excavations at Saraçhane in Istanbul*, Vol. II (Princeton: Princeton University Press, 1992)

Henderson A., "SS. Sergius and Bacchus, Constantinople," *The Builder* 90 (1906), 7–8

Hill S. J. , "The Brickstamps," in (Harrison, 1986), 207–225

Hill S. J., "Review of Harrison 1989," *JHS* 111 (1991), 252–253

Hill S. J., *The Early Byzantine Churches of Cilicia and Isauria* (Aldershot: Hampshire Variorum, 1996)

Hodges R., "Review of Harrison 1986," *AJA* 92/3 (1988), 458–459

Humphrey J. H, F. B. Sear, and M. Vickers, "Aspects of the Circus at Leptis Magna," *Lydia Antiqua* 9–10 (1972/73), 25–97

James L., "'And Shall These Mute Stones Speak?' Text as Image," in L. James (ed.), *Art and Text in Byzantium* (Cambridge: Cambridge University Press, 2007), 188–206

James L. and R. Webb, "To Understand Ultimate Things and Enter Secret Places," *Art History* 14 (1991), 1–17

Kaegi W. E., "Review of Harrison 1989," *JNES* 53/1 (1994), 50–51

Kakko V. E., *Die Gebälkstücke der frühbyzantinischen Hagios Polyeuktos in Istanbul. Zur Rekonstruktion der Exedren des Naos*. M.A. Thesis. (Freiburg: Universität Freiburg, 2011)

Kiilerich B., "Reconsidering the Figural Marble Panels Found in St. Polyeuktos, Constantinople," in A. M. D'Achille, A. Iacobini, P. F. Pistilli (eds.), *Domus sapienter staurata. Festschrift Marina Righetti* (Milan: Silvana Editoriale, 2021), 38–46

Kleiss W., "Bemerkungen zur Kirche Johannis des Täufers in Istanbul-Bakirköy (Hebdomon)," in E. Akurgal and U. B. Alkim (eds.), *Mélanges Mansel* (Ankara: Türk Tarih Kurumu Basimevi, 1974), 207–219

Kleiss W., "Grabungen im Bereich der Chalkopratenkirche in Istanbul," *IstMitt* 16 (1966), 217–240

Kleiss W., "Neue Befunde zur Chalkopratenkirche in Istanbul," *IstMitt* 15 (1965), 149–167

Koder J., "Imperial Propaganda in the Kontakia of Romanos the Melode," *DOP* 62 (2008), 275–291

Koder J., "Justinians Sieg über Salomon," in Θυμίαμα στη μνήμη της Λασκαρίνας Μπούρα (Athens: Benaki Museum, 1994), 135–142

Koder J., "Review of Harrison 1989," *JÖB* 41 (1991), 367–368

Krautheimer R., "Again Saints Sergius and Bacchus at Constantinople," *JÖB* 23 (1974), 251–253

Krautheimer R., *Early Christian and Byzantine Architecture* (Baltimore: Penguin Books, 1965)

Krautheimer R., "Response to Deichmann 1972," *BZ* 65 (1972), 446–448

Krueger D., "Christian Piety and Practice in the Sixth Century," in M. Maas (ed.), *Cambridge Companion to the Age of Justinian* (Cambridge: Cambridge University Press, 2005), 295–315

Kudde E., *Stoudios Manastır Kompleksi – Ioannes Prodromos Kilisesi (İmrahor İlyas Bey Camii – İmrahor Anıtı) Koruma Projesi ve Önerileri* (Istanbul: Fen Bilimleri Enstitüsü, 2015)

Kudde E., "The Construction and Architectural Characteristics of the Monastery," in E. Kudde, N. Melvani, and T. Okçuoğlu (eds.), *Stoudios Monastery in Istanbul: History, Architecture and Art* (Istanbul: Koç University Press, 2021)

Lafontaine J., "Review of Harrison 1989," *Byzantion* 60 (1990), 565–568

Leatherbury S. V., *Inscribing Faith on Late Antiquity: Between Reading and Seeing* (London: Routledge, 2020)

Lowden J., *Early Christian and Byzantine Art* (London: Phaidon, 1997)

Macrides R. and P. Magdalino, "The architecture of ekphrasis: Construction and context of Paul the Silentiary's poem on Hagia Sophia," *BMGS* 12 (1988), 47–82

Maguire H., "The 'Half-Cone' Vault of St. Stephen at Gaza," *DOP* 32 (1978), 319–325

Mainstone R., *Hagia Sophia: Architecture, Structure and Liturgy of Justinian's Great Church* (London: Thames and Hudson, 1988)

Mainstone R., "Structural Analysis, Structural Insights, and Historical Interpretation," *JSAH* 56/3 (1997), 316–340

Mamboury E., (1951) "Le fouilles byzantines à Istanbul et ses environs et les trouvailles archéologiques faites au cours de constructions ou des travaux officiels et privés depuis 1936," *Byzantion* 21 (1951), 425–459

Mango C., *Architettura bizantina* (Milan: Electa, 1974)

Mango C., "Isaurian Builders," in P. Wirth (ed.), *Polychronion. Festschrift Franz Dölger* (Heidelberg: C. Winter, 1966) 358–365

Mango C., "Notes d'épigraphie et d'archeologie Constantinople, Nicée," *Travaux et Mémoire* 12 (1994), 343–358

Mango C., "Review of Harrison 1986 and Harrison 1989," *JRS* 81 (1991a), 237–239

Mango C., "Review of Harrison 1989," *Apollo* 133 (1991b), 348

Mango C., "Storia del arte," in A. Guillou (ed.), *La civiltà bizantina dal IV al IX secolo. Aspetti e problemi, Università degli Studi di Bari Centro di Studi Bizantini, Corso di Studi 1* (Rome: L'Erma di Bretschneider, 1977), 289–350

Mango C., "The Church of Sts. Sergius and Bacchus Once Again," *BZ* 68 (1975), 385–392

Mango C., "The Church of the Saints Sergius and Bacchus at Constantinople and the Alleged Tradition of Octagonal Palatine Churches," *JÖB* 21 (1972a), 189–193

Mango C., *The Art of the Byzantine Empire 312–1453: Sources and Documents* (Englewood Cliffs: Prentice-Hall, 1972b)

Mango C., "The Date of the Studios Basilica at Istanbul," *Byzantine and Modern Greek Studies* 4 (1978), 115–122

Mango C., "The Origins of the Blachernae Shrine at Constantinople," in N. Cambi and N. Marin (eds.), *Acta XIII Congressus Internationalis Archaeologiae Christianae, Split-Porec 25.9.–1.10.1994*, Studi di Antichità Cristiana 54 (Vatican City: Pontificio Istituto de Archeologia Cristiana, 1998), 2.61–76

Mango C. and E. J. W. Hawkins, "Additional Finds at Fenari Isa Camii, Istanbul," *DOP* 22 (1968), 177–184

Mango C. and I. Ševčenko, "Remains of the Church of St. Polyeuktos at Constantinople," *DOP* 15 (1961), 243–247

Marinis V., "Church Building and Ecclesiastical Practice," in S. Basset (ed.), *The Cambridge Companion to Constantinople* (Cambridge: Cambridge University Press, 2022), 180–199

Mathews Th. F., "Architecture et liturgie dans les premiers églises palatiales de Constantinople," *Revue de l'art* 24 (1974), 22–29

Mathews Th. F., *The Early Churches of Constantinople: Architecture and Liturgy* (London: University Park, 1971)

Mathews Th. F., "The Palace Church of Sts. Surges and Bacchus in Constantinople," in J. J. Emerick and D. Mauskopf (eds.), *Archaeology in architecture: Studies in honor of Cecil L. Striker* (Mainz: P. von Zabern, 2005), 137–142

Mathews Th. F., "The Origins of Icons," in E. Schwarz, ed., *The Oxford Handbook Byzantine Art and Architecture* (Oxford: Oxford University Press, 2021), 21–29

Mathews Th. F. and N. E. Muller, *The Dawn of Christian Art in Panel Paintings and Icons* (Los Angeles: The J. Paul Getty Museum, 2016)

Mauskopf Deliyannis D., *Ravenna in Late Antiquity* (Cambridge: Cambridge University Press, 2010)

McKenzie J., "The Architectural Style of Roman and Byzantine Alexandria and Egypt," in D.M. Bailey (ed.), *Archaeological Research in Roman Egypt*, Journal of Roman Archaeology Supplement 19 (Ann Arbor: Journal of Roman Archaeology, 1996), 140–142

McKenzie J., *The Architecture of Alexandria and Egypt, 300 BC–AD 700* (New Haven: Yale University Press, 2011)

Megaw A. H. S., "Notes on Recent Work of the Byzantine Institute in Istanbul," *DOP* 17 (1963), 333–372

Meier H.-R., *Spolien. Phänomene der Wiederverwendung in der Architektur* (Berlin: Jovis Verlag GmbH, 2020)

Meier M., *Das andere Zeitalter Justinians. Kontingenzerfahrung und Kontingenzbewältigung im 6. Jahrhundert n. Chr.* (Göttingen: Vandenhoeck &Ruprecht, 2003)

Meier M., "Σταυρωθεὶς δι' ἡμᾶς – Der Aufstand gegen Anastasios im Jahr 512," *Millennium* 4 (2007), 157–237

Meier M., *Justinian. Neue Wege der Forschung* (Darmstadt: Wiss.- Buchgesellschaft, 2011)

Melling M., "Archaeology in Asia Minor," *AJA* 69 (1965), 133–149; *AJA* 70 (1966), 139–159; *AJA* 71 (1967), 155–174; *AJA* 72 (1968), 125–147; *AJA* 73 (1969), 203–227; *AJA* 74 (1970), 157–178

Mendel G., *Catalogue des sculptures grecques, romaines et byzantines*, Vol. 1– 3 (Istanbul: Arkeoloji Müzeleri, 1914)

Mercati G. (1923) "Due nove memorie di S. Maria delle Blachernae," in *Atti della Pontificia Accademia Romana di Archeologia*, Memorie, Ser. 3, Vol. 1 (Roma: Edizioni Quasar, 1923/24) 26–34

Milner C., "The Image of the Rightful Ruler: Anicia Juliana's Constantine Mosaic in the Church of Hagios Polyeuktos," in P. Magdalino (ed.), *New Constantines* (Aldershot: Variorum, 1994) 73–81

van Millingen A., *Byzantine Churches of Constantinople: Their History and Architecture* (London: Macmillan, 1912)

Moffatt A. and M. Tall, *Konstantinos Porphyrogennetos: The book of ceremonies*, Byzantina Australiensia 18 (Canberra: Australian Association for Byzantine Studies, 2012)

Moran N. (2005) "The Choir of the Hagia Sophia," *Oriens Christianus* 89 (2005), 1–7

Moser S. (2012), "Archaeological Visualization: Early Artifact Illustration and the Birth of the Archaeological Image," in I. Hodder (ed.), *Archaeological Theory Today*, 2nd ed. (Cambridge: Polity Press, 2012), 292–322

Müller-Wiener W., "Byzanz und die angrenzenden Kulturkreise," *JbÖB* 31/1 (1981), 575–609

Müller-Wiener W., "Eine neuentdeckte Kirche aus der Gründungszeit Konstantinopels," *Studien zur spätantiken und byzantinischen Kunst* 1 (Bonn: Habelt, 1986)

Nathan G. S., "'Pothos tes Philoktistou': Anicia Juliana's Architectural Narratology," in U. Betka and J. Burke (eds.), *Byzantine Narrative Papers in Honour of Roger Scott* (Melbourne: Australian Association for Byzantine Studies, 2006), 433–443

Nauerth C., *Agnellus von Ravenna. Untersuchungen zur archäologischen Methode des ravennatischen Chronisten* (Munich: Arbeo-Gesellschaft, 1974)

Nauerth C., *Agnellus von Ravenna. Liber Pontificalis. Bischofsbuch*, Vol. I+II (Freiburg: Herder, 1996)

Nees L., "The Iconographic Program of Decorated Chancel Barriers in the Pre-Iconoclastic Period," *Zeitschrift für Kunstgeschichte* 46 (1983), 15–26

Nelson R. S., "High Justice: Venice, San Marco, and the Spoils of 1204," in P. Vocotopoulos (ed.), *Byzantine Art in the Aftermath of the Fourth Crusade: The Fourth Crusade and Its Consequences* (Athens: Academy of Athens, 2007), 143–151

Nelson R. S., "The History of Legends and the Legends of History: The Pilastri Acritani in Venice," in H. Maguire and R. S. Nelson (eds.), *San Marco, Byzantium, and the Myths of Venice, Dumbarton Oaks Byzantine Symposia and Colloquia* (Washington, DC: Dumbarton Oaks Research Library and Collection, 2010), 63–90

Olcay Uçkan B. Y. and G. K. Öztaşkin, "Olympos Excavations 2018," *ANMED* 17 (2019), 222–231

Olcay Uçkan B. Y., G. K. Öztaşkin, Ö. E. Öncü, S. Evcim, and M. Öztaşkin, "Olympos Kazisi 2017 Yili Çalişmalari," *KST* 40/3 (2019), 617–638

Ousterhout R., "Aesthetics and Politics in the Architecture of Justinian," in C. Morrisson and J.-P. Sodini (eds.), *Constantinople réelle et imaginaire*, TM 22/1 (Paris: Association des amis du Centre d'histoire et de civilisation de Byzance, 2018), 103–120

Ousterhout R., *Eastern Medieval Architecture: The Building Traditions of Byzantium and Neighboring Lands* (Oxford: Oxford University Press, 2019)

Ousterhout R., "New Temples and New Solomons: The Rhetoric of Byzantine Architecture," in P. Magdalino (ed.), *The Old Testament in Byzantium* (Washington, DC: Dumbarton Oaks Research Library and Collection, 2010), 223–253

Ousterhout R., "Review of Bardill 2004," *BZ* 98 (2005), 575–577

Ousterhout R., "Study and Restoration of the Zeyrek Camii in Istanbul: First Report, 1997–98," *DOP* 54 (2000), 265–270

Ousterhout R., "The Sanctity of Place and the Sanctity of Buildings: Jerusalem versus Constantinople," in B. D. Wescoat and R. Ousterhout (eds.), *Architecture of the Sacred* (Cambridge: 2012, Cambridge University Press), 281–306

Parment T. W., *An Alternative Reconstruction of the Church of St. Polyeuktos in Istanbul*. M.A. thesis. (State College: Pennsylvania State University, 1999)

Parpulov G. L., "Review of Mathews and Muller 2016," *Plekos* 21 (2019), 59–64

Parpulov G. L. and L. A. Schachner, *From the Bosporos to Oxford: Unseen Photographs of Prof. Harrison's Byzantine Excavations in Istanbul* (Oxford: Oxford University Research Archive, 2012)

Pasquini Vecchi L., "La scultura di S. Polieucto. Episodio saliente nel quadro della cultura artistica di Constantinopoli," *RSBS* 1 (1999), 109–144

Pentcheva B., *Hagia Sophia: Sound, space, and spirit in Byzantium* (State College: The Pennsylvania State University Press, 2017)

Perry M., "Saint Mark's Trophies: Legend, Superstition, and Archaeology in Renaissance Venice," *Journal of the Warburg and Courtauld Institutes* 40 (1977), 27–49

Perry S., *The Archaeological Eye: Visualization and the Institutionalization of Academic Archaeology in Britain*. Ph.D. dissertation. (Southhampton: University of Southhampton, 2011)

Peschlow U., "Altar und Reliquie. Form und Nutzung des frühbyzantinischen Reliquienaltars in Konstantinopel," in M. Alltripp and C. Nauerth (eds.), *Architektur und Liturgie* (Wiesbaden: Reichert, 2006), 175–202

Peschlow U., "Dekorative Plastik aus Konstantinopel an San Marco in Venedig," *Makedonika* 5 (1983), 406–417

Peschlow U., "Die Johanneskirche des Studios," *JÖB* 32/4 (1982), 429–435

Peschlow U., "Observations in the so-called Skevophylakion of Ayasofya in İstanbul," *AST* 26/2 (2008), 391–393

Peschlow U., "Review of Harrison 1989," *Gnomon* 65/7 (1993), 627–630

Pizzone A. M. V., "Da Melitene a Costantinopoli: S. Polieucto nella politica dinastica di Giuliana Anicia. Alcune osservazioni in margine ad AP 1.10," *Maia* 55 (2003), 127–132

Preger Th., *Scriptores Originum Constantinopolitanarum* (Leipzig: Teubner, 1901)

Prinzing, G., "Das Bild Justinians I. in der späteren Überlieferung der Byzantiner vom 7. bis 15. Jahrhundert," *Fontes Minores* 7 (1986), 1–99

Puig I. Cadafalch J., A. de Folguera, and J. Goday y Casals, *L'arquitectura Romànica a Catalunya 1. L'arquitectura Romana. L'arquitectura cristiana preromànica* (Barcelona: Institut d'Estudis Catalans, 1909)

Restle M., "Konstantinopel," *Reallexikon zur byzantinischen Kunst* 4 (1990), 366–737

Restle M., "Krypta," *Reallexikon zur byzantinischen Kunst* 5 (1995), 454–484

Rhoby A., "Byzantinische Kirchen als Orte der Interaktion von Wort, Bild und Betrachter. Inschriften im sakralen Kontext," in W. Eck and P. Funke (eds.), *Öffentlichkeit – Monument – Text, XIV Congressus Internationalis Epigraphiae Graecae et Latinae, 27.–31. August* (Berlin: De Gruyter, 2014), 650–652

Rotman T., *Hagiography, Historiography, and Identity in Sixth-Century Gaul: Rethinking Gregory of Tours* (Amsterdam: Amsterdam University Press, 2022)

Runciman S., "Preface," in R. M. Harrison (ed.), *A Temple for Byzantium: The Discovery and Excavation of Anicia Juliana's Palace-Church in Istanbul.* (Austin: University of Texas Press 1989), 8

Russo, E., "Costantinopoli. Architettura e scultura dei primi secoli," in T. Velmans (ed.), *Bisanzio, Costantinopoli, Istanbul* (Milan: Jaca Book, 2008), 39–108

Russo E., "Evidence from the Theodosian Saint Sophia," in C. Barsanti and A. C. Guiglia (eds.), *The Sculptures of Ayasofya Müzesi in Istanbul: A Short Guide.* (Istanbul: Ege Yayınları, 2010), 19–34

Russo E., "Il lapidario di Ayasofya a Istanbul. Le sculture architettoniche della chiesa di S. Sofia Teodosiana," in R. Martorelli (ed.), *Itinerando Senza confini dalla preistoria ad oggi. Studi in ricordo di Roberto Coroneo* (Perugia: Morlacchi editore, 2015), 301–324

Russo E., "Introduzione ai capitelli di S. Sofia di Costantinopoli," *RIASA* 67 (2012), 95–172

Russo E., "La decorazione scultorea della S. Sofia teodosiana di Constantinopoli," *Bizantinistica Rivista di Studi Bizantini e Slavi* 2/9 (2007), 1–14

Russo E., "La scultura di S. Polieucto e la presenza della Persia nella cultura artistica di Constantinopoli nel VI secolo," in A. Carlie (ed.), *Atti del Convegno internazionale "La Persia e Bisanzio". Rome 14–18 ottobre 2002* (Rome: Accademia Nazionale dei Lincei, 2004), 737–826

Russo E., "The Sculptural Decoration of the Theodosian Church of St. Sophia," *AST* 26 (2009), 155–166

Russo E., "Un capitello constantinopolitano a Ravello," in U. M. Fasoa (ed.), *Quaeritur inventus colitur: Miscellanea in onore di Padre Umberto Maria Fasola 2*, (Vatican City: Pontificio Istituto di archeologia cristiana, 1989), 671–695

Saccardo G., "I Pilastri acritani," *Archivio Veneto* 34 (1887), 285–309

Scheja G., "Hagia Sophia und Templum Salomonis," *IstMitt* 12 (1962), 45–49

Schlunk H., "Byzantinische Bauplastik aus Spanien," *MM* 5 (1964), 234–254

Schneider A. M., "Die Blachernen," *Oriens* 4/1 (1951), 82–120

Schneider A. M., "Die vorjustinianische Sophienkirche," *BZ* 36 (1936), 77–85

Schneider A. M., *Die Grabung im Westhof der Sophienkirche zu Istanbul* (Berlin: Deutsches Archäologisches Institut, 1941)

Ševčenko I., "Note additionnelle [Les trouvailles de Saraçhane (Istanbul) et l'église Saint-Polyeucte]," in J. Lafontaine, 'Fouilles et découvertes byzantines à Istanbul de 1952 à 1960', *Byzantion* 29–30 (1959/60), 386

Shahîd I., "The Church of Hagios Polyeuktos: Some New Observations," *Graeco-Arabia* 9/10 (2004), 343–356

Shahîd I., "The Church of Sts. Sergios and Bakchos in Constantinople: Some New Perspectives," in A. Avramea, A. Laïou, and E. Chrysos (eds.), *Byzantium, State, and Society: In Memory of Nikos Oikonomides* (Athens: Institouto Byzantinon Ereunon, Ethniko Hidryma Ereunon, 2003), 467–480

Sherry L. F., *The Hexameter Paraphrase of St. John, Attributed to Nonnus of Panopolis: Prolegomenon and Translation*. Ph.D. Dissertation (New York: Columbia University, 1991)

Singes J., "Archivo gráfico de España y la Peninsula ibérica VI: El periplo de un capitel bizantino en España," *SEB* 9 (2011), 3–10

Smith J.-Ch., "Review of Harrison 1989," *JSAH* 51/2 (1992), 216–217

Sodini J.-P., "Les paons de Saint-Polyeucte et leurs modèles," in I. Ševčenko (ed.), *Aetos: Studies in honour of Cyril Mango* (Leipzig: Teubner, 1998), 306–313

Sodini J.-P., "Remarques sur les briques timbrées de Constantinople," *REB* 63 (2005), 225–232

Speck P., "Juliana Anicia, Konstantin der Große und die Hagios Polyeuktos in Konstantinopel," *PB* 11 (1991), 133–114

Spieser J.-M., "Review of Harrison 1986," *Bulletin Monumental* 148 (1990), 326–328

Stadtmüller H., *Anthologia Graeca VI: Epigrammatum Palatina Cum Planudea* (Leipzig: Teubner, 1894)

Stanzl G., *Längsbau und Zentralbau als Grundthemen der frühchristlichen Architektur* (Wien: Verlag der Österreischer Akademie der Wissenschaften, 1979)

Stroth F., *Monogrammkapitelle: Die justinainische Bauskulptur Konstantinopels als Textträger* (Wiesbaden: Reichert Verlag, 2021)

Strube Ch., *Die westliche Eingangsseite der Kirchen von Konstantinopel in justinianischer Zeit* (Wiesbaden: O. Harrassowitz, 1973)

Strube Ch., *Polyeuktos und Hagia Sophia. Umbildung und Auflösung antiker Formen, Entstehen des Kämpferkapitells* (München: Verlag der Bayerischen Akademie der Wissenschaften, 1984)

Strzygowski J., *Kleinasien. Ein Neuland der Kunstgeschichte* (Leipzig: J. C. Hinrichs, 1903)

Taddei A., *Hagia Sophia before Hagia Sophia: A study of the Great Church of Constantinople from its origins to the Nika Revolt of 532* (Rome: Campisano editore, 2017)

Talbot Rice D., *Art of the Byzantine Era* (London: Thames and Hudson, 1997)

Talbot A.-M., "Patronage of Byzantine Churches and Monasteries," in R. A. Etlin (ed.), *The Cambridge Guide to the Architecture of Christianity I* (Cambridge: Cambridge University Press, 2020), 166–175

Tantsis A., "The So-called 'Athonite' Type of Church and Two Shrines of the Theotokos in Constantinople," *Zograf* 34 (2010), 3–11

Tavano S., "La restaurazione Guistiniania in Africa e nel alto Adriatico," *Aquileia e l'Africa Antichità Altoadriatiche* 5 (1974), 251–283

Terry A., "Review of Harrison 1989," *JAAR* 63/3 (1995), 623–626

Thiel A., *Die Johanneskirche in Ephesos* (Wiesbaden: Dr. L. Reichert Verlag, 2005)

Tigler G., "I pilastri 'acritani': genesi dell'equivoco," in G. Trovabene (ed.), *Florilegium atrium: Scritti in memoria di Renato Polacco*, Miscellanea 8 (Padova: Il poligrafo, 2006) 161–172

Toivanen H.-R., "The Church of St. Polyeuktos: Archaeology and Texts," *Acta Byzantina Fennica* 2 (2003/4), 127–150

Tronzo W., "Reading the Display of Sculpture on the Façade of San Marco in Venice," in M. Gianandrea, F. Gangemi, and C. Costantini (eds.), *Il potere dell'arte nel Medioevo. Studi in onore di Mario D'Onofrio* (Rome: Campisano Editore, 2014), 725–733

Tunay M. İ., "Byzantine Archaeological Findings in Istanbul During the Last Decade," in N. Necipoğlu (ed.), *Byzantine Constantinople: Monuments, Topography and Everyday Life* (Leiden: Brill, 2001), 217–231

Veh O., *Bauten. Prokop. Beschreibung der Hagia Sophia, Paulos Silentiarios: Griechisch-Deutsch* (München: Heimeran, 1977)

Vickers M., "A Sixth-century Byzantine Source for a Venetian Gothic Relief in Vienna," *DOP* 33 (1979), 335–336

Vickers M., "A 'New' Capital from St. Polyeuktos (Saraçhane) in Venice," *OxfJA* 8 (1989), 227–230

Vickers M., "Review of Harrison 1986 and Harrison 1989," *Antiquity* 64 (1990b), 693–694

Vickers M., "Wandering Stones: Venice, Constantinople, and Athens," in K.-L. Selig and E. Sears (eds.), *The Verbal and the Visual: Essays in Honor of William S. Heckscher* (New York: Italica Press, 1990a), 225–242

Viermann N., "Surpassing Solomon: Church-building and Political Discourse in Late Antique Constantinople," in M. K. Konstantin and J. Wienand (eds.), *City of Caesar, City of God*, Millennium Studies 97 (Berlin: De Gruyter, 2022), 217–241

Vogt A., *Constantin VII Porphyrogénète, Le Livre des Cérémonies*, Vol. 2 (Paris: Les Belles Lettres, 1935)

Warmebol E., "Review of Hayes 1992," *Latomus* 55/3 (1992), 745–746

Westphalen S., *Die Basilika am Kalekapı in Herakleia Perinthos. Bericht über die Ausgrabungen von 1992–2010 in Marmara Ereğlisi*, Istanbuler Forschungen 55 (Tübingen: Ernst Wasmuth Verlag, 2016)

Whitby M., "The St. Polyeuktos Epigram (AP 1.10): A Literary Perspective," in S. F. Johnson (ed.), *Greek Literature in Late Antiquity: Dynamism, Didacticism, Classicism* (Aldershot: Ashgate, 2006), 159–188

Whitby M., "The Vocabulary of Praise in Verse-Celebrations of Sixth-century Building Achievements: AP 2.398–406, AP 965, AP 1.10 and Paul the Silentiary's Description of St. Sophia," in D. Accorinti and F. Vian (eds.), *Des Géants à Dionysos. Mélanges de mythologie et de poèsie grecques offerts à Francis Vian* (Alessandria: Edizioni dell'Orso, 2003) 593–606

Wilkinson J., "'Paulinus' Temple at Tyre," *JÖB* 32/4 (1982), 553–561 [= Akten II/4, XVI. Internationaler Byzantinistenkongress]

Wolf G., "Marble Metamorphosis," in D. Gamboni, G. Wolf, J. N. Richardson (eds.), *The Aesthetics of Marble from Late Antiquity to the Present* (Munich: Hirmer, 2021), 14–61

Cambridge Elements ≡

The History of Constantinople

Peter Frankopan

University of Oxford

Peter Frankopan is Professor of Global History at Oxford University, where he is also Director of the Centre for Byzantine Research and Senior Research Fellow at Worcester College. He specialises in the history of the Eastern Mediterranean from antiquity to the modern day, and is the author of the best-sellers *The Silk Roads: A New History of the World* (2015) and *The New Silk Roads: The Future and Present of the World* (2018).

About the Series

Telling the history of Constantinople through its monuments and people, leading scholars present a rich and unbiased account of this ever-evolving metropolis. From its foundation to the domination of the Ottoman Empire to contemporary Istanbul, numerous aspects of Constantinople's narrative are explored in this unrivalled series.

Cambridge Elements ☰

The History of Constantinople

Elements in the Series

The Statues of Constantinople
Albrecht Berger

The Hippodrome of Constantinople
Engin Akyürek

The Church of St. Polyeuktos at Constantinople
Fabian Stroth

A full series listing is available at: www.cambridge.org/EHCO